MW01078277

Inspire People to Greatness

The Reeves Connection Method

How to Connect Through Personal Conversation as Taught by an Interrogator

Edition 1, 2017

Author: Dale Norman Reeves, CFI

Editor: Anna Reeves

Copyright © 2017 Dale Norman Reeves, Integrity Talks LLC

All rights reserved.

No part of this book may be reproduced or transmitted in any form or by any means whatsoever, including written, electronic, recording, or photocopying, without express written permission from the author, except by a reviewer who may quote brief passages to be printed in a magazine or newspaper. Please refer all pertinent questions to the author at reevesconnectionmethod@outlook.com. Dale Norman Reeves, CFI.

Chapters

One: The Process of Connecting   Page 1

Two: **The Three Do Nots**   Page 27

Three: 1. Relating   Page 31

Four: 2. Opinions and Advice   Page 45

Five: 3. Judging   Page 71

Six: **How to Connect**   Page 83

Seven: 1. Extraordinary   Page 97

Eight: 2. Very Important Moment   Page 109

Nine: 3. Virtues and Values   Page 143

Ten: 4. Listen and Lead   Page 197

Eleven: 5. Acknowledge   Page 211

Twelve: Putting it all together   Page 217

Acknowledgements   Page 232

Inspire People to Greatness

The Reeves Connection Method

How to Connect Through Personal Conversation as Taught by an Interrogator

Most people say that what they really want to accomplish in their lifetime, is to make a difference in other people's lives. This book will give you the tools so that you can make a difference in people's lives every day, no matter where you are or what you are doing. Not only will you be able to make a difference in people's lives, but you'll also inspire them to greatness! How can you make a difference in people's lives and inspire them to greatness? That's what the rest of this book is about.

Let me introduce myself. I am a CFI, Certified Forensic Interviewer, otherwise known as an interrogator. I have interviewed and interrogated hundreds of people resulting in hundreds of confessions from those who have

committed crimes. I own a company called Integrity Talks.
I conduct seminars and provide training that helps
individuals and teams learn how to make meaningful,
honest connections through conversation. When people
connect, the results are amazing!

I also work for a large corporation, conducting
investigations and performing interrogations. Because I
work for a large corporation, I must be concerned not only
about solving crimes, but also about maintaining and
building positive relationships within the company.

Communication is essential in my job, and leading everyday
conversation into a connection helps me build
relationships. I need to be approachable so people will
communicate with me if they witness a theft happening
within the corporation.

Knowing how to listen and what to listen for enables me to
tell if someone is being truthful or deceptive. Being able to
tell the difference between truth and deception is essential
in my job. I also listen for what is behind the words people
are saying.

When listening for what is behind the words other people
are saying, I am able to discern what motivates them. As an
interrogator, I listen for motives. How do I find someone's

motive? I listen for the virtues and values that are behind people's words in order to find their motives. The motive is what motivated them to commit the crime.

Leaders tell me that one of their biggest challenges at their job is knowing how to motivate people. Once you learn how to listen for virtues and values, you will know how to motivate others. You will be able to inspire others.

I developed the Reeves Connection Method, through years of study and practice, as a way to connect with people during an interrogation. I then discovered this method was useful in nearly every other aspect of my life. This method of communication has brought me great success in my business conversations and also in my personal life.

Everyone loves it when a conversation turns into a connection. However, most people don't know how to make this happen. I have trained teams and individuals in the Reeves Connection Method and they have found new success in their business and personal lives.

I will share a step-by-step strategy that will allow you to communicate in any and all circumstances. This method of communication has given me peace and confidence in high conflict conversations. It has also given me the skills to be able to communicate in a way that is touching and inspiring to people - even to criminals!

In the pages of this book I am going to share with you a communication secret I learned from my experience as a CFI. This is a successful strategy I've developed for powerful communication. I will share stories of some of my interrogations to demonstrate this method. Of course, I will change the names to protect the privacy of those involved.

These principles will unlock the skills you already possess. I believe you already have the skills you need to be an effective communicator. The fact that you have picked up this book tells me that you are an amazing person who cares about communication. We all have a desire to communicate effectively.

I have observed that most of us have fallen into old habits of ineffective communication passed down to us through generations of people trying to survive and do the best they can. No matter how hard most of us have worked to fix our communication, we've continued to get the same results. Most individuals I speak to, tell me they struggle and get frustrating outcomes while communicating with some of the most important people in their lives.

I study each interrogation I conduct. I spend hours preparing for an interrogation and I spend hours reviewing the interrogation after it's completed. I analyze the results of every interrogation I conduct. I calculate that I've spent over 10,000 hours studying for, reviewing and conducting conversations for the interrogations I perform. As a result of my study, I have discovered five things that create a connection. I have also discovered three things that destroy a connection. I was not very good at connecting in my first few interrogations, but I am an expert now.

Imagine if you had recorded most of the major conversations you've had at your job. You reviewed them, summarized the conversations and wrote them down. Then you studied the conversations and determined what needed improvement and what was effective at accomplishing your goals. Then you asked others who sat in on each conversation what their thoughts were about how it went. At that point you calculated what could have improved the conversation. Eventually, you'd be an expert at communication.

I'm not asking you to study each of your conversations, but that is how I have studied my profession. Learning how to create understanding is a rewarding skill to have. By reading this book, and applying its principles, you can take advantage of all that I have learned. You can discover how to connect effectively with another person through conversation.

Often, conversations turn into a battle of wills. In many conversations, such as employer to employee, parent to child, business negotiations or in many interrogations, there is a battle of each person's will, with a winner and a loser. The Reeves Connection Method changes conversations from a win-lose battle to a win-win resolution. Both sides have the satisfaction of feeling a mutual win-win result in the conversation.

I don't know about you, but when I was growing up I never received any training on how to have a personal conversation. I learned how to write and give a speech in school, but there was no training about how to connect with other people in a meaningful way.

In college I took speech classes, but there weren't any courses on how to have an effective personal communication with someone. Most of us just learn by the trial and error method. Maybe we met someone once and liked how they spoke so we tried to emulate them. Or maybe our parents gave us advice regarding our communication by saying things such as, "Don't say that, because it's rude."

Some of us may have learned some communication techniques in therapy after having a disastrous relationship. Most of us improvise and learn how to communicate as we go through life. The problem is, we find out that we're often misunderstood. We have a hard time connecting with people in conversations, let alone motivating and inspiring them to greatness.

The difficulty with learning as we go is that we're going to leave behind a trail of destruction in our relationships. With the trial and error method, we are going to have a lot of error. After experiencing failure we may withdraw from connecting with others or worse yet, settle for superficial, 'safe,' but unsatisfying relationships.

Even though I won't teach you how to interrogate people in this book, I will give you an easy to follow method to have a powerful connection during a conversation. A powerful connection is essential in an interrogation. Through this book you can gain the knowledge it took me thousands of hours to perfect.

Although this book is not about how to interrogate people, this is the most important thing I've learned to have success in interrogations.

As a CFI, I interview and interrogate people. An interview is when I am asking questions and having a conversation with someone in order to distinguish truthful behavior from deceptive behavior. The interview turns into an interrogation when I have ascertained that the person I am interviewing has deceptive behavior and has committed an offense against the company or another individual.

(If you want to learn about truth and deception, or learn how to be an interviewer and an interrogator, I suggest you attend the classes and take the courses offered by Wicklander-Zulawski at www.w-z.com.)

The information I am going to share with you is applicable to leaders, managers, diplomats, sales people, teachers, fathers and mothers, customer service professionals, doctors, lawyers... Whatever profession you have, you can benefit from learning how to connect with people!

The Reeves Connection Method is not a method of interrogation. It is, however, a method to connect with another person in a one-on-one conversation. Connection is a necessary part of the interrogations I conduct. I've also learned that forming a connection with another person during a conversation is an essential part of everyday communication.

I am a person who gets things done. I like to make an impact in a short time. By reading this book and applying its principles, you will see that the Reeves Connection Method is brief and impactful. By using this method you will be able to develop a connection with people in just a few minutes.

It's my suggestion that you consider setting aside everything you've learned about communication and consider the new method I am going to share with you.

I have a request. Most of us have talked and walked for years and we may have developed some habits that we think are good. Everyone has some good communication habits. But, ask yourself, "Are my communication habits brief and impactful? Do they inspire people to greatness? Do they build the kind of relationships I want to build?"

If not, let's mentally set those habits aside for now. When you've read this book and tried the Reeves Connection Method, you can always go back to comunication as usual if you desire.

You will find some useful and enlivening habits here that you can incorporate into your life. These skills will give you a far higher level of satisfaction and success in both business and personal communication.

Let me first define the Reeves Connection Method. Many people tell me that the first thing that comes to their minds, when they hear the word connection, is a social media connection or a cell phone connection. This connection is not at all like that, rather it is a personal deep connection between two people. The Reeves Connection Method is about gaining an understanding between two people. When I speak with others, they often say, "Finally, someone who gets me! Finally someone who understands me!"

This method makes people feel understood and it also inspires them to greatness. When you apply the Reeves Connection Method to your conversations you will not only inspire others, but you will also be moved to create your own possibilities of greatness.

My definition of greatness: When someone recognizes the potential, confidence and ability they possess. And this recognition enlivens them and inspires them to make a contribution to the world and a difference in people's lives.

There are three things that kill a connection. These are three things that we do almost every day in our conversations. You may be shocked to learn what they are.

After clearing away these connection-blockers, I will walk you through the five-step connection process.

During a conversation you will be able to go through the five steps to connection in just a few moments. You will learn how to quickly inspire people. During your conversation you will be able to understand the value the person you're speaking with brings to the world and you will be able to recognize them for their contribution. You will see the virtues and values the other person has, that are behind the words they are speaking. You will learn what motivates the other person. In the Reeves

Connection Method you are going to learn how to listen to what's behind the words you are hearing.

You can use the Reeves Connection Method to teach people how to give extraordinary customer service. By learning this method and teaching your team how to listen, what to listen for and how to truly connect with a customer, you can turn your customer service into something amazing. You will actually be able to speak with grouchy customers and inspire them to greatness. It's really amazing to see people's transformation from grouchy to happy. Most businesses don't have a conversation method for customer service. You will have a method to teach your team after reading this book.

When I interview and interrogate people, it means there probably has been a crime committed. For example, when a pharmacy is missing a bottle of narcotics, I interview all the people who work at the pharmacy. During these interviews I watch body language. I watch and listen for energy at certain moments. I listen for qualifiers and modifiers. There are dozens of things I listen and watch for. When I am finished with the interview I can tell if the person sitting across from me has committed the crime or if they are innocent.

I interrogate human beings. Human beings deserve respect, even when they have done something they shouldn't have. When I connect with the person sitting across from me I am able to get a confession, while at the same time leaving them with their dignity. My interrogation method is not at all like what you see on TV. I do not yell and threaten with statements like, "I know you did it! Now confess, because you're doing time!"

I developed this method of connection because I felt it was important for each person I interviewed to be respected as a human being. Not all methods of interrogation leave people with their dignity and a feeling of being respected. Although most methods of interview and interrogation work really well, sometimes both the innocent and the guilty people feel disrespected and upset after being interviewed.

The Reeves Connection Method, instead, causes people to be honest with me and therefore they willingly confess to the crime they have committed. They envision the person they really want to be, with the virtues and values they desire to have. In other words, I inspire them to greatness! A lot of people I interrogate express relief at finally having told someone the truth. They discover hope for their future.

Once you learn how to inspire people to greatness your conversations become motivating. I use this method of inspiring people to greatness in everyday conversations and you can do the same. All you need is a desire to transform your communication into something powerful.

I have had amazing results. As I have started teaching the Reeves Connection Method to others, they have had similar results. After an hour of training in a group setting one man, a leader in his community, said, "This is everything I've always desired to be! Now, I have a method to get there."

Another leader said, "I'm going to college. I have learned more in one hour with you than I have learned in weeks of college classes with my professors!"

People often tell me, "I'm a better person when I'm around you." By using the Reeves Connection Method you can have this same effect on people.

This method is not only about what we say and how we listen, but how and what we think about other people.

The real substance in this book can be summed up in the following two paragraphs:

You are going to create something with your moments instead of waiting around to see what happens. Yes, you are going to learn how to create a conversation instead of waiting to see how it goes. You will learn how to take control of a conversation by letting the other person communicate to you. And through the steps of the Reeves Connection Method, you will inspire them to greatness!

Basically, if you don't know how to listen intently, you won't be successful in communicating your thoughts! I'm not listening to people so I can resonate to them on their level. Instead, I am listening to them so I can bring them toward my thoughts. I'm connecting to them on my level, not on their level. Remember, it's my goal to inspire them.

To develop the Reeves Connection Method, the first thing I had to realize was that listening is the greater part of communication. Imagine an interrogator that didn't listen! They wouldn't be very successful. Likewise, if you don't know what to listen for in a conversation, you won't be very successful in communicating that special concept that you want the other person to understand. A successful interrogator listens very intently. They listen for details. The interrogator listens for certain parts of the conversation so they know when to move on to the next step of the conversation.

For a lot of people, the word 'listen' isn't neutral, but it reminds them of accusations from their childhood, "You don't listen to me." "Sit still and listen." And, "Why aren't you listening?" I had to shake off any negative connotation the word 'listen' had for me. Now, I understand that listening is the key to a connection that transforms situations. But you can't just listen to someone and let them ramble on. I have a method for listening. Listening is a very assertive action. It is not passive.

Some people like to use the word 'hear' because hearing means you apprehend or comprehend what the other person is saying. But I use the word 'listen' because you are not trying to hear what they saying. You are listening for something they are *not* saying. You are listening for and distinguishing the meanings that lay behind what they are actually saying. You are perceiving the virtues and values they possess.

For example, when someone is upset and they use words that sound mean and nasty, we might hear things we don't like. But if we listen deeply we might see someone who simply likes things to be perfect, or at least fair. Or, if we listen deeper, we might possibly see that they are just afraid. Once you've discerned that someone is afraid, instead of unpleasant, it transforms the whole moment.

There have been times my wife was upset with me. It used to cause an argument because I saw her as angry and accusatory. But now I listen for what is behind the words being spoken. I can simply see that sometimes she is afraid of our relationship drifting apart. So I simply say, "Honey, you value closeness and partnership. I love that. You are my dream come true. If I ever do anything as stupid as leaving you, I want you to come and drag me back home. You are my home. I want to be close to you." Her unpleasant words don't affect my mood because I am listening to understand the virtues and values behind the words she is speaking.

This changes the whole moment and she smiles at me and it draws us closer together instead of putting a wedge between us. In other words, we are inspired to greatness in our relationship. Instead of struggling through another day with each other, we are delighted to be together.

Through this method of communication, we can learn *not* to take things personally. The other person might be yelling. But when you learn to listen for *what is not being said*, you clearly see that the yelling is not directed at you. <u>Rather, it is simply a virtue or value the other person is struggling to explain.</u>

Possibly, you are like I was in the past and right now you have a relationship that is in some sort of conflict. Maybe you are having conflict with a spouse, child, sibling, neighbor or someone at work. No matter how hard you try to explain things and convince people that you have good thoughts for them, they misunderstand you.

I was in a similar place at one time. Everything changed for me when I developed and applied the Reeves Connection Method to my relationships. Now my life is unrecognizable from what it was in the past. My goal is that you will experience something similar.

Let me start with a story that shows some of the technique.

I was investigating a case where we were missing $75,000. We were completing an audit and found that five years earlier we were missing about a thousand dollars a day for 75 days. The theft had taken place over five years before our investigation began! I thought to myself that the person who took this money probably felt pretty good about not getting caught after this much time had passed.

During our investigation we found out that Alice, one of the bookkeepers, had worked each and every day the money was missing. The police were going to arrest her, because all of the evidence pointed to her. That's a pretty reasonable conclusion. We thought the mystery was solved. However, I wanted to interview Alice and get a confession from her before having the police come in and talk with her. I sat down with Alice and started the interview.

During our conversation I used the Reeves Connection Method as my conversation and connection model. I thought of Alice as an extraordinary person, I thought of the moments we were talking to each other as very important. I searched for her virtues and values and I listened and led the conversation. I acknowledged Alice for the values I found in her. It didn't take me long to come to the conclusion that Alice didn't take the money. Her behavior was honest and truthful. Even though all of the evidence pointed to Alice, it was evident to me that she was innocent.

The other bookkeeper, Mary, had not worked during the days the money was missing; or at least Mary hadn't clocked in during the days in question. We decided to interview her anyway. It didn't take very long for me to see that it was clear that Mary was the one who had taken the money.

When I asked about the missing money, numerous times, Mary said she didn't take it. I used the interrogation methods I learned as a CFI to determine truthful from deceptive behavior. One time, during our conversation, I asked her, "Mary, did you take the money?" She shook her head yes, but said, "No." This is a classic deceptive response, and it happens more often than you would expect. Mary still couldn't bring herself to confess to the crime.

Finally, I decided to use the five-step Reeves Connection Method during the interview. I created Mary as an extraordinary person. I created and thought of this moment as a very important moment. I aimed my listening to search for Mary's virtues and values. I listened and led the conversation and I acknowledged her for the virtues and values that I found. I saw that Mary had a deep love for her family and spent her free time volunteering in her community. I discovered that behind what Mary was saying were the virtues of family and love.

I said to Mary, "Mary, you are an extraordinary person. This moment is very important. You have the virtues and values of family and love. This money-thing is not who you are. I see how this is tearing at your being. You are family and love. The stress of worrying about this has probably taken months, if not years, off of your life. This is not who you are."

The tension on Mary's face instantly drained and she looked relieved. She said, "You are right. My family says I'm not fun anymore. I took the money. I am so glad you came in today to talk to me. This is a huge relief."

After we discussed what was going to happen next, Mary said to me, "So many times I have tried to tell my husband what I did. I wanted to tell my boss at work about the money I took, but I just couldn't get the words out. I've tried to have integrity, but I just couldn't bring myself to say what I wanted to say."

She told me, "You see something in me that allows me to be the person I long to be. You see the real me better than I ever saw myself."

The police came into the room and arrested Mary for the crime she committed. While Mary was walking down the hall with the police she stopped, turned around and looked at me. She called back to me and said, "Thank you for helping me today. You saw something in me today that I had forgotten about. I'm grateful for our conversation."

After Mary stole money from the company her fear was that people would see her as a criminal. I saw Mary as an extraordinary person who had made a bad choice. When I recognized Mary for her virtues and values of family and love, she felt compelled to tell me exactly what she'd done. She didn't say, "I am family and love." I saw family and love behind the words Mary was speaking. That's what you are going to learn to do in this book. You will learn to recognize the virtues and values behind what people are saying.

Why would Mary thank me after she was arrested for a crime? I believe it's because of how I spoke to her and the method I used. I inspired her to greatness. I inspired her to be honest and face the consequences, whatever the consequences might be.

Mary's inspiration didn't only last for 24 hours. Over the next two years Mary paid back all the money she took from the company.

Many times, when we are inspired, the inspiration only lasts for a day or two. We may hear an inspirational story in a sermon on Sunday, but by Monday we've forgotten about it and we return to life as normal. This is because the inspirational story we heard was about someone else, it wasn't about us.

Through the Reeves Connection Method, people are inspired by their own virtues and values. They are inspired by their own story. Therefore the inspiration is lasting and profound, not short lived.

Many people have thanked me after they confessed to a crime and while they were being arrested. This may sound surprising, but each of them were thankful for being recognized for their unique virtues and values.

I discovered that if I can connect with a person in the intense setting of an interrogation, I can use some of the same technique in every day communication to build quick and lasting connections with my family, friends and acquaintances.

Imagine a world where everyone connected! If I can bring connection to some of the most confrontational conversations, then you can help me bring it to the world, one conversation at a time.

What would it be like if people at work could connect and be a real team? What would it be like if leaders of countries could connect and understand each other? What would it be like for you if you connected with your children?

What would it be like for you, if after a conversation, your teenager said this to you? "Thank you for listening to me today! You saw something in me today that I had forgotten about. I am grateful for our conversation."

I use The Reeves Connection Method every day with many people I meet. Now I want to share this method with you.

First, I will talk about three things I had to clean up in my listening and conversations in order to make this method effective. Imagine a closet full of clothes. If you bought three new shirts and put them in a closet that was packed full of clothes, the new shirts would become wrinkled immediately. But if you removed some old clothes from the closet, the new clothes would perform as you intended them to perform. Likewise, we will get rid of a few habits of listening that interfere with connection and we will clean up some of our thoughts about conversations.

Some of the habits of conversation that I had to get rid of are conversation techniques I actually *learned* at business conferences and sales trainings. I was *taught* to use some of these techniques. But I have learned that these three habits damage the connection in a conversation. At one time I thought these habits were pretty helpful during a conversation, habits such as relating. Yes, we are going to get rid of relating to people. I know it sounds crazy, but in the chapter about relating, you will easily see why relating is a barrier to connection.

This is where some people say, "What? I was taught to relate to people. I use relating every day." Please stay with me here. After reading the relating chapter, you will understand what relating really does to a conversation. You will actually understand how damaging relating can be to a connection.

Then I will go through the five steps of the Reeves Connection Method. The amazing part of this method is that you will discover you already have the skills to connect. It takes years of study to be an effective interrogator, but you will be able to apply this method and inspire people to greatness immediately after reading this book.

About 20 years ago I said to a co-worker, "I don't play the politics game at work."

He responded, "Oh, yes you do. Everyone plays. By not playing, you're playing."

That wasn't what I wanted to hear from him, but I had to agree in my mind that he was right.

Likewise, everyone plays in the connection part of communication. Everything we say has an impact. Even the things we don't say have an impact. You can't win by not being involved. You can't win unless you communicate to win. We all play in the arena. Some of us feel as though we are fighting an uphill battle. We feel like we can't win. Let's start winning and connecting.

Dale Reeves

The Three Do-Not's

Let's talk about the three habits we need to clean up in order to make space for true connection.

I am going to ask you to add five skills to your communication habits later in this book. But for now, let's get rid the Three Do-Not's:

Do not relate.

Do not give opinions or advice.

Do not judge.

You might be thinking, "What are you talking about? I don't judge people. I don't give unwanted opinions or advice." And in your opinion you are right. But we are going to take a look at how your conversations might be perceived by others. If someone *feels* judged by you, you've lost the chance to inspire them.

Think about a time when you felt judged during a conversation. This might not have been the intention of the person you were speaking with. Nonetheless, you felt judged and therefore you probably weren't very inspired.

In the next three chapters we will focus on relating, giving opinions or advice and judging. If you stop doing these three things, connecting with another person during a conversation will be a possibility instead of a dream.

I can't only do the five steps of connection, I have to make sure I *don't* do these three things. If I were to complete all five steps of connection, but related, gave opinions or advice, or made a judgement during my conversation, I would not be able to make an effective connection.

Please understand that you can relate, give opinions and advice and judge people if you want. All of these things are good at certain times and all are necessary parts of life and of communication. But if your desire is to make a connection that inspires people to greatness, you must not do these three things. If I want to get a confession, I cannot do these three things.

I'd prefer not to start the Reeves Connection Method with a list of negative connection-blockers. After all, we are learning how to inspire people to greatness. But I firmly believe that we need to understand our communication habits and the negative effect they may be having on our ability to connect with others. Each of the Three Do-Nots were part of my communication habits at one time. I thought they were good habits until I discovered how destructive these three habits were. I was shocked. I think you will be too.

Dale Reeves

One: Do Not Relate

(The Three Do-Nots)

Do not relate. This is difficult to understand at first. Usually, we think we *should* relate to people. We've been taught to relate to people. But relating narrows the conversation down to a specific topic.

For example, if I said, "Where are you from?" And the other person said, "Utah." If I was from Utah, I could relate and say, "Hey, I'm from Utah too." And then, what would we talk about? We'd talk about Utah.

See. Relating narrows the conversation down to what two people have in common. I had one man say to me, "But then we can have a conversation about something we both know something about." Really? How boring. You just took thousands of possible topics and narrowed it down to only one, Utah. Just because both of you are from Utah doesn't mean you have a connection. Are you connected to everyone else who lives in the same state as you? Of course not. But for some reason, we feel as though relating to the subject of living in the same state is something special that will create a connection.

People will talk if you let them and they will tell you all sorts of things. People will speak about what troubles them and they will talk about their needs and their triumphs if you ask the right questions.

But when you relate to someone, you limit the subject to a very narrow topic, and they won't tell you about their troubles and their triumphs. You actually lose their attention. Your conversations will end as a very 'nice' unproductive chat that tastes a little bitter. The conversation will be without connection. And without connection you do not have the other person's heart and mind. Without connection you are simply two people, unconnected, going your separate ways.

As an interrogator, I cannot narrow the conversation down to a single topic. I have to leave it open so the suspect will take me to where they want to go, or maybe to where they don't want to go. They will get to the interesting part of the conversation, as long as I don't narrow it down to a single topic. When I decide I want to zero in on a topic, only then will I relate to them. But relating is actually a controlling tactic.

When we say, "Hey, me too, I'm from Utah." We are sort of forcing the other person to talk about Utah. It would seem strange for the other person to say, "Hey, how about those Cubs." After you said, "Hey, me too, I'm from Utah." (Because the Cubs are from Chicago, Illinois.) No. They would feel forced, or manipulated, to talk about Utah. The other person may play along, and it may seem like you have a very nice conversation about Utah. But more than likely, you won't experience a true connection through this relating conversation.

We may not like to think about it this way, but relating is actually a *very forceful controlling tactic*. If we relate we get to talk about a topic we know something about. Either consciously or unconsciously we may be controlling the topic so we have something comfortable to say. We may even subconsciously use relating to *avoid* meaningful connection or to keep someone at a comfortable distance.

I have had many conversations with people who said they grew up on a farm, but I don't tell them I also grew up on a farm. Why? Because we would narrow the topic down to growing up on a farm. I would have missed out on the real substance and value of the conversations I've had with people. It may be fun to talk about growing up on a farm, but relating to the topic would have nothing to do with inspiring them to greatness.

I used to forget the name of someone I just met, five seconds after they introduced themselves to me. This was because I was looking for something to relate to. Then I would miss some of what they were saying to me, because I was thinking of how I could ask them for their name again, without embarrassing myself. Maybe I'd hear them say something about Hawaii. When I'd hear something I could relate to, I'd say something like, "Yeah, me too! I went to Hawaii two years ago and I really liked snorkeling."

Not only did I forget their name, but now I just stole their thunder. I interrupted them while they were telling me about their trip and I told them about my trip. Really, who cares if the both of us went to Hawaii?

Then I would get up the nerve to ask them their name again. I would be clever and say it like this, "How do you spell your name?" And they'd say, "M-A-R-Y." Now I really felt uncomfortable and embarrassed. Have you ever have a conversation like that?

I don't relate to people when I want to make a connection. Since I'm paying attention, I usually remember the names of the people I meet. People's names are important to them.

We will remember people's names if we aren't thinking of what to say. Don't worry about what to say. Listen. Be truly interested in them as a person. We will learn how to listen and lead the conversation in step four.

I've seen this anonymous quote. "Possibly our greatest accomplishment in the day could be keeping our mouth shut about ourselves."

During a conversation our minds flash pictures and words in our heads about the things we've done. Our minds are trying to relate and make sense of what the other person is saying.

Our minds take short cuts and our minds are trying to help us out by flashing things in our heads that we can relate to. Just ignore the pictures and words for a little while. Just because something pops up in your head doesn't mean you have to say it. If we said everything that pops up in our minds we'd probably have a hard time keeping a job or keeping a relationship. This is a really important concept of connection.

I remember being at a conference and the speaker suggested that we could remember names by simply relating a person's name to something similar. The example he gave was, if a man's name is Mr. Salmon, think of him as looking like a fish. The next time you see him you can say, "Hi, Mr. Salmon."

I was always worried that if I tried to remember a man's name by imagining him looking like a fish, I would call the man Mr. Carp or maybe Mr. Halibut. I was always too afraid to try that method.

Imagine if your name was Mr. Smith, and I thought I could remember the name Smith by relating it to a simple or easy name to remember. Then I said, "Hi, Mr. Simple," or "Hello, Mr. Easy?" This is not a good method for me.

In communication, relating takes the emphasis off of the other person and it basically says, "Hey, look at me! I did the same thing!" <u>Relating distracts the other person and changes what they were going to say.</u>

I was watching TV one night and a singer-songwriter said, "The next song I am going to sing is about my dad. I wrote this song last week. My dad died two weeks ago." The MC of the show interrupted him and said, "I know how that feels. I lost my dad two years ago." The singer-songwriter hesitated uncomfortably. Then he started to play his guitar and sang his song.

It was easy for me to see that the singer-songwriter had more he wanted to share with his audience. But when the

MC said, "Hey, me too," it changed the moment and it distracted the singer-songwriter from the message he meant to share. If he had been allowed to share, uninterrupted, he may have had a message that would have resonated in a meaningful way with his audience.

Relating kills the moment. Relating takes the attention off of the other person and puts all the attention on yourself. And maybe that's where you want the attention. Maybe you want it on yourself. However, if you want to connect to someone, or inspire someone, you want the attention to be on them. So I suggest we don't steal their moment. Let's not make it all about ourselves. Let the other person talk and see where it goes. It's a lot more fun and inspiring when we don't relate.

Here's an example of how relating usually works: You're telling me about your trip to Florida. You're getting ready to tell me about an interesting experience you had. You start talking about it and the picture of a trip I once took to Florida pops into my head. So I relate and say, "Hey! I went to Florida once too. I rented a car and it broke down so they gave me an SUV. I loved it. I like that you can sit up a little higher." How would that relating conversation make you feel? This conversation would not inspire anybody. It would not bring a connection.

You see, just because someone else *mentioned* Florida, all of a sudden the picture I have of Florida pops into my head. And just because a picture pops into my head and I'm having a conversation with you, I feel as though I have to comment on the picture in my head. Because I've been taught to relate, I may think this is good. That's how relating often works. We never realize the damage relating does, and all that we miss.

If I was conducting an interrogation and the topic came up of the other person's trip to Florida, I would want to know about their trip. I would not relate to them because I want them to lead me to the next part of the conversation.

Here's another example. Maybe you want to tell me about your child who wrote you a poem while he was in the hospital, and he thought he was dying. If I tried to relate and said, "Yeah, I love it when kids write poems! I remember one time when I was gone for a week at work and my child wrote me a poem. You're right. That is special." How would this conversation make you feel?

Instead of relating I could say, "Tell me about the poem. I'm sure that was a frightening time."

These might seem to be extreme examples, but I've heard worse. Much worse! This is what we do when we relate.

When we relate we actually damage the relationship. When we relate we never get to hear the important thought the other person had on their mind. We don't realize the damage we just did to the conversation because we don't know what they were trying to share with us.

I was 14 when my 10-year-old sister, Dawn, died. I remember standing at the funeral home as people came in to pay their respects to my parents.

I remember one person, not understanding, said, "It is going to be okay. You'll forget about her soon."

Another person said to my parents, "I lost my daughter. I know how you feel. Stay strong and don't think about it too much."

Someone said to me, "I lost my sister too. I know how you feel."

None of this made us feel any better. These people related and gave advice. They shared their opinions.

The only thing that gave us any comfort was the people who said, "I can't imagine what you are going through! I'm here for you if you need anything." I'm sure everyone who came to visit meant well. They just didn't know that relating doesn't help. Relating actually hurts.

Someone once told me that relating was a kind thing to do because it gave the other person something to talk about. But actually, it gives *you* something to talk about. The other person is already talking. I would rather think that people are powerful and wonderful and that they have something intelligent to say if I give them a chance.

Let's see our children as powerful and exceptional. Let's give them a chance to talk. And let's see others as having something to say.

Don't narrow the conversation down to what you have in common. If you always relate, you'll rarely learn something new from the people you meet. You'll miss out on so much.

In the world of interrogation, the person with the knowledge has the power. If *I* know how *they* think, I have more power. If I relate, then *they* will know how *I* think, and the power will switch back to them. Listening will give you power. Just listen. Learn something about the other person. Gain the knowledge about what they have to say. You don't have to prove you're smart too. You don't have to prove anything. Listen and don't relate.

What do we talk about then, if we can't relate? I'll tell you more about that later in step four. Step four is about listening and leading. When I listen and lead, I make the other person look good. When I relate to people I am attempting to make myself look good. (Making ourselves look good, through relating, doesn't bring about meaningful connection. Actually, relating doesn't make anybody look good.)

Listen and lead says, "Tell me more about your trip to Hawaii. What was your favorite part? If you ever went back to Hawaii, what would you do differently?"

Relating says, "I went to Hawaii too. I like the beach. It's so much fun. You know, next time I go, I would like to climb that mountain that I could see from the beach."

A lot of people go to Hawaii on vacation. Just because someone else went there, doesn't mean you have a connection. And it doesn't mean this is a good time to talk about your experiences in Hawaii. If you want to talk about Hawaii, go ahead. But realize, relating your experience of going to Hawaii may stop the flow of what they were trying to tell you. Maybe they were trying to tell you something, and talking about Hawaii was only the beginning of what they wanted to say. <u>Diverting someone from their thoughts won't inspire them to greatness.</u>

Listening and leading is all about making the other person look good. Relating puts the focus on yourself and your story. Once you understand this concept and you listen to conversations other people are having, you'll notice people battling for air time. Each person is in a battle trying to share their own story. While listening to other people battle for air time I end up thinking, "I used to do that." Now I'm glad I understand the damage relating does to a conversation.

I will be sharing my experiences in this book, and by the end of the book, I hope you will clearly see how relating kills a connection. In the examples I give, if I had related instead of connecting, I would not have received the same amazing results!

Think about spending a few moments with your favorite actor, actress or sports star. Would you relate to them? Or would you be enthralled, simply by their presence? I doubt you'd share your trip to Los Angeles with them, just because that is where they live.

I don't think you'd relate your story of coaching little league to your favorite baseball player. You'd probably listen and lead naturally. You might say something like, "Tell me what it feels like to be a professional athlete. How much time do you spend in the weight room?" Or, "What was it like to be in the World Series?" You might say something like, "I remember when you hit that home run in the World Series.

We were screaming on the couch watching you run the bases. You were so calm and cool, without any expression, as you were running the bases! Wow that was awesome!"

You may ask your favorite actor or actress, "Which movies have you enjoyed acting in the most? What's it like watching a movie you were in? What was your first job in this career?" You probably wouldn't share your experience in the high school play.

Treat people as though they are famous. You will see them light up. They will enjoy the time they spend with you.

Seriously, if you had a desire to date someone in particular, you wouldn't steal the attention from them by relating to them. You'd ask them about themselves and let them look good. Once they see you are truly interested in them, they may give you their phone number. If you're not getting many phone numbers, maybe you're relating a little too much.

Someone once said to me, "Maturity is when I have the chance to make it all about me, but instead I choose to let someone else shine."

If you are like I was at one time, you may find yourself thinking at first, "I can't believe relating is so destructive. I do it all the time. It is my communication style."

Don't worry, after reading the entire book and learning what to replace relating with, it will make perfect sense.

Two: Don't Give Opinions or Advice

(The Three Do-Nots)

The chapter on relating can be difficult to understand at first. But after reading the last chapter on relating, I hope you're beginning to understand that relating actually destroys a connection.

Likewise, this chapter on opinions can be difficult to understand too. But really, it's fairly simple. What we're doing here is getting rid of some conversation habits that we may have taken for granted as being natural or good.

Sometimes we think that our opinions are who we are. We have this thought that our personality is built on the opinions formed about everything we have learned so far in life. Therefore, our opinions can feel very personal to us. Some people may believe that their opinions define who they are.

It's a great thing to have opinions, however, opinions draw a line in the sand. Opinions separate us. If you want to connect with someone, you don't want to be separated from them. The words *connection* and *separation* are in opposition to each other.

I am not saying you should never share your opinion. But if your desire is to connect with someone, then you should consider holding your opinion back. There are ways to share your opinion and still keep a connection, once the connection has been made. But first we must make a meaningful connection.

If your desire is to share your opinion and engage in a debate with others, that's your choice. It can be a wonderful thing to debate differing opinions and in some cases it's important. Different ideas and opinions help us solve problems. It's essential to listen to other's ideas and opinions, and then share our own ideas and opinions.

And of course, it's important to speak up when someone is being treated unfairly. In those cases it's *very important* to share your opinion.

There are effective ways to share your opinions if your desire is to be understood. Shouting out your opinion during a debate may feel like fun, but it will not create understanding. This book is not about how to have a debate. I will briefly talk about how to effectively share your opinion. But the key to being effective in sharing your opinion is to first make a connection.

Think back to a time when you shared your opinion with someone who had a different opinion than yours. Maybe it was a political opinion. How did that go for you? Were you understood? Did you create a connection with others? Did sharing your opinion create a deep relationship with the people you spoke with?

You may feel that your opinion inspires you. But when you share your opinion, it may not inspire others. If your desire is to connect with someone, keep your opinions to yourself. I know this sounds rather harsh, but stay with me. People really aren't interested in your opinion. They're really not. They're not really interested in my opinion either.

Opinions are usually built on some sort of virtue or value. When someone else shares their opinion, the last thing they want to hear is your opinion, if it's in disagreement with theirs. This is because your opinion shuts their opinion down. And remember, they may feel that their opinion is a reflection of their values and who they really are. Their opinion is probably very personal for them.

When you share your opinion directly after someone else shares their opinion, you are likely to create misunderstanding. You might be trying to engage in a neutral conversation about the pros and cons of a subject, but that may not be what the other person hears. What they actually hear may shock you.

If your opinion is different than their opinion, what they may hear from you is, "I don't like your virtues and values." And therefore, the line in the sand is drawn! The other person is trying to be heard and they don't want to be shut down. They definitely don't want their values attacked. When you share your opinion, you run the risk of attacking the other person's values.

This is made more complex, because most people become used to not being heard or understood. Sometimes people bring up something controversial in order to build a wall between themselves and you. They know you'll share something that opposes them and they are ready to defend their position. If they can get a wall built, then they can prove that you don't care about them.

During an interrogation, I make sure I don't give the other person any ground to build a wall upon. In an interrogation, if a wall gets built between the suspect and the interrogator, it can be difficult to get a confession.

People ask me, "How can I connect with someone, then? What are other people interested in?" That's the question we need to ask ourselves. You see, opinions are about us. My opinion is about me and what I think. Your opinion is about you and what you think.

Just like we learned in the last chapter. When I relate, I make the conversation about me. And if I want to connect, I need to make the conversation about the other person. Likewise, when I share my opinion, I make it all about me. If I desire to connect with someone, I need to make sure that I don't make it all about me.

Basically, what other people are interested in is this:

"Do you really care about me?"

"Are you really listening to me?"

"Do you understand me?"

"Do you care about my virtues and values?"

When I listen to another person's opinion and I don't share mine, what should I do? I need to listen for their virtues and values, (which you will learn to do in Step 3 of How to Connect.) I search for the virtues and values behind their opinion. I listen for what is behind the words they are saying.

I had a man come up to me at a break during one of my training sessions and say to me, "But opinions are personal, how can I listen to their opinion without sharing mine?"

I responded, "You are absolutely correct. Opinions are personal. That's the reason you need to keep your opinion to yourself if you want to connect with someone."

He said, "I guess that's right. I see that if I share my opinion then I make it all about me. But aren't I agreeing with them if I don't speak up?"

I said, "If you feel it's more important to share your opinion than to connect with someone, then by all means, share your opinion. Sometimes sharing your opinion can be the best thing to do."

He said, "So I need to decide if I want to share my opinion or connect with someone, right?"

I responded, "Yes, that's right. But remember, it's your job to inspire them. In order to inspire them, you need to connect with them first. In the Reeves Connection Method you will be leading the conversation. If you respond to someone's opinion, then you are allowing *them to lead* the conversation."

He said, "Wow! I never thought of it like that. So, when I respond to someone's opinion, I'm giving them control?"

"That's right," I said.

I continued, "When I see the virtues and values behind another person's opinion, I am able to comment on something that does not oppose them. I let them know how much I admire the virtue and value behind their opinion. That doesn't mean I agree with their opinion. It just means that I value the other person more than I value their opinion."

He said, "I get it. I see that this will make a big difference in my life."

When I recognize the virtues and values behind someone's opinions and thoughts, and then I acknowledge them for those virtues and values, they feel understood. They feel as though I care about them and I see value in them. (Which I actually do.) I search for the virtue and value behind their opinion. This is not manipulation. Instead, I see new beauty in the world! I don't have to agree with their opinion to see this beauty. I am discovering virtues and values that I admire.

I focus on people's virtues and values, not on their opinions.

Once they know I admire their virtues and values, and that I see worth in who they are, I've created connection instead of separation between us. What I've actually done is, I have not allowed them to build a wall between us.

After the other person clearly sees that I admire the virtues and values behind their opinions, then they may begin to ask me about my opinion. But if I bring up my opinion too early in the conversation, I will build a wall between the two of us. They will feel opposed. They will never be inspired by someone who opposes them and doesn't recognize the values they hold. In fact, they won't be interested in anything I have to say!

So how do you share your opinion when you need to? Sometimes you have to share your opinion, such as at a business meeting or at a city council meeting. It's okay to share your opinion, but make sure you acknowledge the virtues and values of the other people who've spoken first. This will defuse a possible argument. It makes others feel like their contributions are valued. After someone has been recognized for the virtues and values that lay behind what they are saying, they are more apt to listen to your opinion. Instead of feeling silenced, angry and opposed, they will be listening to you. You'll be creating understanding, instead of disagreement!

In personal conversations, business meetings and interrogations, I share my opinion when I *need* to. I just make sure I recognize the other person for the virtues and values they possess first.

It's fairly easy to connect with someone who has the same opinions we do. We get to complain about the same things and cheer for the same things. However, I am sharing how to connect with *anyone and everyone*, not just those who share the same opinions as ours.

How do we connect with people who have different opinions? We must keep our opinions out of the conversation.

Let's talk about where opinions come from. What are opinions anyway? Where do we get our opinions? If we can define what an opinion is and where it comes from, maybe we can see how an opinion can damage a connection.

Let's do an exercise:

Let's imagine we're taking out a piece of paper. Next, imagine you're writing down the following things:

Write down each school you've ever attended. Start with grade school, middle school, high school and then college.

Then write down each teacher you ever had. Start with each grade school teacher, middle school teacher, high school teacher and college professor.

Write down every coach or scout leader you've had.

Write down every art or music professional you've ever taken a lesson from.

Now write down each class you've taken in school or after school. Include tech school and college classes.

Now write down the name of each person you ever spent a day with.

Then write down every city or town you ever lived in or visited overnight.

Having some trouble remembering? That's okay. Just write down as many as you can recall. Most of us can't even remember many of the things we've done.

Some of us have trouble remembering a teacher's name. Why? We spent an entire year with them, or at least a semester. We said and heard their name hundreds of times. I know I can't recall every teacher I had.

Okay, take a look at your list. Ask yourself this question, "Is there anyone else in the world who has had the same experiences I've had? Is there anyone else with the exact same list?"

We have to come to the conclusion that nobody is exactly like you. Nobody has had the same experiences you've had and they can't possibly understand what you've been through. They can't possibly know what you think about every moment of the day. Your list is different than anyone else's. Therefore, your opinion is going to be different than anyone else's. At least the reason for your opinion will be different.

Each one of us is unique.

Teachers are very important. Many people say that there was a special teacher who made a huge difference in their life. They say this special teacher changed their direction and made them who they are today.

College classes give us knowledge and change what we think about economics, nutrition and science. College classes can give us a direction in life for a career.

Vacations can give us an experience outside of our normal world. Trips can give us a new perspective on things.

We haven't even written down religious differences or politics. What if we added that to the list?

Everyone is different. We can't even begin to understand every reason why people act the way they do. Good friends and family members with similar experiences sometimes vote differently in elections. Something has caused them to draw different conclusions.

Each one of us is exceptional. Nobody has the same orientation as you or me. We should all expect to have different perspectives and opinions. Therefore, we should all expect to be misunderstood.

That's right! We should *expect* to misunderstand the person we're listening to! And we should *expect* them to misunderstand us.

Expect communication to be misunderstood. It's not a big deal. If we can expect to be misunderstood, then we can ask for clarification. We can say, "Tell me what you understand about what I just said."

And then we can ask for clarification about what they said by saying. "I want to make sure I understand what you just said. This is what I understand…"

I had someone in one of my seminars come up to me afterwards and say, "I get it. I'm crazy if I get upset over someone having a different opinion. Wow! This is life-changing!"

Most of us would probably agree that we think our opinions are right and opposing opinions are wrong.

Sometimes people get upset over misunderstandings and say things like, "Oh, you just don't get me. You don't understand." But the struggle is simple. People have different opinions because they have a different background and they've had different experiences.

Now I think it's no big deal if we have a difference of opinion. In fact, I expect others to have a different opinion than mine. And yes, I'd love to hear their opinion.

If we can expect to have different opinions, we can see difference as normal. Possibly we can see difference as fascinating. Maybe we don't need to fear an idea that's different than ours.

I'm simply saying that we should not think we are victims of other people's opinions, just because their opinions are different than ours.

Again, I don't expect others to have the same opinions I do. When I give my opinion, I expect someone else to have a different opinion. It is clear to me that when I want to connect with someone, I should not bring up our differences.

Years ago I used to have misunderstandings almost weekly with my boss. I finally realized I was absurd thinking we should naturally understand each other. I grew up milking cows on a farm and he grew up in a major city. To resolve this conflict, I simply made a request. I asked my boss if I could get all of his expectations in writing. He sent them to me. I went back to him and we discussed them. Wow, what a difference! He's an amazing leader when I understand him. And now, if my boss and I have a misunderstanding or a difference of opinion, I'm not all bent out of shape over it. I take 100% responsibility to solve the problem by asking for clarification.

There is a lot of peace in any relationship when we know how to create understanding.

The Reeves Connection Method brings us together. I can have a connecting conversation with people that have different opinions than mine. Imagine if I was only successful with people who shared my opinions. I wouldn't get many confessions.

It shows maturity in life when we can hear different opinions and be okay with it. Some people close others out of their lives because of a difference in opinion. Opinions can be strong. However, most of our opinions are due solely to our circumstances and life experiences. And as we found out in our little exercise, no one is exactly like you. Of course people will have different opinions!

Even if we've taken in all the available scientific data to form our opinion, there still may be a whole realm of scientific data that will be discovered shortly and that will change everything we know about a subject.

My point is only for us to see that we can connect with people who have a different opinion from us. Don't be threatened by other people's opinions! If you had to walk in their shoes for 20 to 40 years or more, maybe you would have drawn the same conclusions they have.

When I perform an interrogation, I have to separate the crime from the person. I can still think the person is extraordinary and amazing, even if they stole something. I have a pretty strong opinion about theft. However that doesn't mean the person who stole is bad. I don't have the opinion that only bad people steal things. I understand that good people can make bad choices. I separate the person from the action.

We put padlocks on doors to keep honest people from making bad choices. Thieves will break in even though a door is locked.

I can still love and believe in my kids even if they did something wrong. I can still love someone if they have a different opinion than mine. I don't want to get ahead of myself here, because we will talk about judging in the next chapter, but opinions are sort of like judgments.

We have to be able to hear someone's opinion without making a judgement about them.

It's my job to get the confession, it is not my job to judge the person who committed a crime. I get a written confession. I call the police and let the police do their job. Then the person who stole something gets to talk to the judge. I am not the judge. I let the judge do their job. To judge is not my job. And likewise, to give them my opinion is not my job. In fact, if I give them my opinion that stealing is wrong, they probably won't confess.

When I want to connect with someone, I make sure I don't give my opinion.

Let's talk about advice. Think about a time when you were down and out. Did you really want another person to come up to you and give you advice at that time? Usually when we're down and out we don't want to hear somebody else's opinion or their advice. So why do we give other people our advice? Giving unwanted advice drives a wedge between people.

Let me tell you a story that explains this. I was having lunch with some business associates. Everyone had finished their lunch and as people were saying goodbye, a 35 year old woman, Susan said, "I hear you're writing a book. What's it about?"

I said, "Let me show you."

And she said, "Okay."

A great way to get a conversation started is to ask someone to tell you about something they did immediately after high school graduation. After finishing twelve years of high school most people feel free and excited. Sometimes they take short trips or embark on some kind of journey they have been thinking about for a long time. It's a time when people often start a new chapter in their lives.

I asked Susan to tell me about something that happened after she graduated from high school.

She said, "I moved to a large city."

I asked, "Where did you graduate from high school?"

Dale Reeves

Susan told me where she attended high school. I know the school! I have had friends and family attend that very same high school! I lived in that same city for four years. I did not relate to her and tell her that I had friends and family that attended the very same school. Relating to her would have changed our entire conversation.

I asked, "Why did you move to the city?"

She told me, "I had a bad relationship with my boyfriend."

"What happened?" I asked.

She said, "My boyfriend ran me off the road with his car."

I said, "Wow that sounds frightening! What did you do then?"

She said, "I called my dad, who lived in the city four hours away, and he came and got me."

"Was your dad there for you when you needed him?" I asked.

She said, "Yeah, I guess he was."

I asked, "So what did you do in the city?"

She said she worked for a while and then went to school for four years.

I asked, "What did you study?"

She said, "Design."

I asked, "What did you do with your degree?"

She went on to tell me about her jobs in various states. She beamed with excitement as she explained her exciting career.

After she was finished I asked her, "So what brought you to this town?"

She said she had finally gotten the dream job of her life. She was in charge of design for a major company. However, only a few months into her job, the economy caused her company to close.

"So what did you do?" I asked.

She replied, "I went back to school and got my degree in teaching and now I'm a grade school teacher."

I asked, "How do you like teaching?"

Tears came to her eyes and she just sat still and silent for a moment. "I hate it!" She finally admitted, "I don't know what to do."

I didn't say anything. I just handed her two napkins from the table so she could dry her tears.

This is the time when most of us would give advice. Right? I could have said, "Well, follow your heart." Or I could have said, "Make sure you use your head and think this out." Or I could have said a lot of things. I mean, she looked like she could use some advice, right? Nope. She didn't need my advice. Besides, I understand that people really don't want advice.

Because I listened, she took me right to where her struggles were. People will do that. If given the chance they'll talk about the most important things they're going through. If you're not hearing people's struggles, you're not listening and leading.

People will get at the heart of their problems and their struggles if we let them. It's not that they need advice, it's just that they have a desire to tell someone so they don't feel so alone in the world.

In most conversations people don't get to the heart of their struggles because we relate to them. Relating narrows the possible subjects down to what you have in common. Had I related to Susan, it would have definitely killed this connection. But because I did not give advice, or relate, she told me her struggles.

After a short time, she looked up at me and said, "Wow! You are a good listener. I just told you two things that I've never told anyone else. Only my parents know my boyfriend ran me off the road and nobody else knows I hate teaching."

She gave me a hug and we parted ways.

I saw her six months later. She came up to me, "Thank you for your advice," she said with a big hug. "I got back into design and I love it." I didn't remind her that I never gave her any advice. Nonetheless, she credited me with her success. It was probably because I listened to her so deeply that she was able to come to a conclusion on her own.

People need someone to listen to them. Had I related to her we would have talked about something completely different. If I related to her it would have been a nice conversation, but we wouldn't have connected. We probably wouldn't have given each other a second thought as we went our separate ways.

It's not that I listen to other people's problems all day long. However, if I want to make a connection with another person, I need to allow the conversation to get a little deeper than just talking about the weather. (Unless I'm speaking to someone who has a burning desire to be a meteorologist.)

When we relate and give opinions or give unwanted advice, we kill our chances of the conversation getting deep enough to make a connection.

Think back to when you were a teenager. Did you want to hear advice from your parents? Most of our teenagers do not want to hear our advice. I ask permission to give advice. When one of my children is talking to me about a problem, I usually just listen. I ask questions and I listen and lead, but I don't give advice. Sometimes I will ask, "Permission to give advice?" If they say no, I will not give advice. When they say yes, I give them my opinion and advice. However, I make sure I ask first.

I want my children to talk to me. I want to be a safe place where they can just talk. Besides, I want to know what's going on. If I give them unwanted advice, they'll quit talking to me and they won't tell me what's going on.

It's not that I let my children struggle without my help or direction. I accept them as they are. I connect with them and allow them to come up with solutions on their own.

I'm not saying I don't make mistakes. This is not a book about parenting. My skills are in connection. There are moments to give advice. Advice can be needed at times and children need direction. If you don't feel as though you connect with your children, possibly it is because unwanted advice kills a connection.

Usually, when a parent gives unwanted advice, teenagers will rebel. Many adults even rebel against unwanted advice. No, *most* adults rebel against unwanted advice.

My first goal is to have a relationship with my children. I only want to love them and admire who they are. My children are smart. They don't want my opinion or advice. If they want my opinion or advice, they will ask for it.

If someone wants your advice they will usually say something like this, "Hey, what do you think I should do with this situation?"

Think about yourself and something you're going through right now. If you told someone about your struggles, it might just be you want to vent. Maybe you want to complain. Possibly you just need to talk about the situation. If you were in the middle of telling about a difficult situation you're going through and the other person interrupted you to give advice, their advice would probably taste a little bitter to you. You may feel frustrated. You are not likely to continue telling them what you're going through.

Opinions and advice need to be kept out of a connecting conversation. Just admire the other person for who they are. Your job is to connect to them. If having a relationship with the other person is more important than having a debate with them, don't share your opinion or give advice.

After I have heard the other person's opinion, and have asked for clarification, usually the other person feels understood. Then they often ask me what I think. If I want to share my opinion at that time I will, but not before being asked.

I had a guy tell me that people get promoted at work because of their opinions and advice. I beg to differ with that statement. Other people tell me that someone who is always giving their opinion and advice is looked at as someone who likes to hear themselves talk. People that get promoted are usually leaders and leaders are usually good listeners. The Reeves Connection Method will help you be a good listener.

In summary: When you give your opinion, you make it all about you and what you know. If you want to connect with someone, keep your opinion to yourself. Focus on the other person's virtues and values that lay behind their opinion. You may not like their opinion, but you can surely admire the zeal, compassion or commitment that is part of their personality.

Regarding advice. Most people don't want to hear advice. Advice usually doesn't set very well with people. If you want to connect with people, don't give advice, unless of course they ask for your advice.

Dale Reeves

Three: Don't Judge

(The Three Do-Nots)

Would you steal a car? Of course most of us wouldn't steal a car. We would agree that stealing a car is bad.

Suppose you drove up into the mountains, found a parking lot near a scenic area, parked your car and went hiking with your spouse or someone you love. While hiking, two guys approach you. They shoot your loved one. Then the two guys steal your cell phones, wallets and keys. You carry your loved one to the parking lot and your car is gone. Obviously, they stole your car. There is no one else in the parking area. You see two other cars in the parking lot and one has the keys in the car. Would you steal that car so you could save the life of your spouse or loved one? Of course you would!

You just went from 'no' to 'yes' in about 30 seconds. Your opinion just changed. You may say, "That's because the circumstances changed." Maybe that's true, but you didn't think of the circumstance before you answered, when I asked, "Would you would steal a car?"

Often we don't think of all of the possible circumstances before we judge someone. We judge people before really understanding. Most of us are guilty of judging people and forming opinions about things, before we look at all the possible situations someone could be facing.

What if nothing's wrong?

That's right. I actually said, "What if nothing's wrong?" Ponder that for a moment.

I saw a young woman, about 20 years old, with bright purple hair. I approached the woman and said, "Your purple hair is amazing! What made you pick the color purple?"

She hesitated a little and acted as if no one had asked her that question before. Then she said, "Well, my grandma used to spend all her money on us. She never liked her hair to be gray, so she would buy the cheapest hair color. It usually turned her hair a little purple."

I commented, "So you color your hair purple in honor of your grandmother?"

She nodded, "Yes."

I said, "Wow. That is amazing! I've never heard of anyone coloring their hair the same color as their grandmother because of their love for her."

I noticed the tattoo she had on her arm. I have come to realize that if someone puts permanent ink on their skin, it usually has a deep meaning. It's usually pretty important to them. So I asked her to tell me about her tattoo.

She rolled up her sleeve, pointed to one part of her tattoo, and told me, "This is when my grandma was born. This part is about her life. This is when she adopted me. And this is when she died."

I was amazed! I was so choked up I could hardly talk. I said, "I want to acknowledge you for your love for your grandmother! I am not sure I've ever seen this much love for a grandma! I am blown away by your love!"

She got a tear in her eye and said, "Thank you."

I said, "So what are you doing with your life?"

She said she was going to college.

I asked, "What are you studying?"

She said, "Business."

I asked, "What do you want to do with your business degree?"

She said, "I want to open an orphanage in honor of my grandma."

Now I felt tears coming to my eyes. I was speechless for a moment. We looked into each other's eyes.

I finally said, "You are incredible! This is the best love story I have ever heard! Thank you for sharing it with me."

She said, "Thank You."

When I started in the security industry, years ago, before getting any training to be a CFI, one man on my team tried to teach me to watch people who dyed their hair bold colors and had tattoos. He told me that, "People like that are shoplifters." How silly. If I had listened to him, I would have judged the incredible young woman with purple hair. I have come to realize that judging people separates us from the world and from other people. When we judge people, we miss so much!

This young woman had designed her entire life around her love for her grandma. This young woman, who I could have judged years ago, has brought me so much joy and hope. It was such a blessing to speak to her for a few moments.

Because of this experience and others, I now understand that a person with tattoos or bold colored hair is not more likely to be a shoplifter than anyone else.

I created the young woman with purple hair as extraordinary and the moment as a very important moment. We were both blessed by the moments we spent talking.

What if nothing's wrong? Instead of looking for what's wrong and judging people, I say to myself, "What if nothing's wrong?" And not surprisingly, I see what is right.

What if purple hair isn't wrong? What if tattoos aren't wrong? What if whatever is bothering you isn't wrong? I was taught that purple hair was wrong. I was taught that tattoos were wrong. But they weren't wrong. These judgments were wrong. How much time has been wasted judging and fretting?! What are you fretting about? Maybe nothing's wrong. Maybe there really isn't anything to fret about.

This is one of the reasons my life has slowed down. I have inspiring conversations with people every day. This makes my life amazing! It's like I get to meet George Washington, Leonardo da Vinci, a woman with purple hair, and Abraham Lincoln in the same day.

My days *are* great because I stop to see people's virtues and values. I don't let people ramble on. I listen for certain things and I lead the conversation, which you will learn in step four. I accomplish more now than I ever have.

I could have easily related to this woman, because my grandma's hair had a bluish-purple tint too. As soon as she mentioned her grandma having purple hair, the picture of my grandma popped up in my mind. I could have said, "Yeah, my grandma's hair used to be purple too. She probably bought that cheap stuff." Had I related to the young woman, she never would have told me her whole story. Instead, because I didn't judge her, I got to hear an amazing love story.

Let's think about relating for a moment. If I had related, we would have talked about our grandmas and how silly their hair looked. When we relate, we give up the chance to connect in a meaningful way. This is the conversation she and I could have had. Neither of us would have felt very good about having a conversation about our grandmothers' silly hair. Had I related, I would have been negating her entire lifelong dream. (Have you ever had a conversation with someone, and after you walked away, told yourself, "That was stupid. Why did I say that?") I am glad I did not relate.

When we relate we give up the chance to inspire people to greatness. The young woman with purple hair inspired me. I am sure she felt inspired to continue with her dream after sharing it with me. I saw a renewed conviction on her face that she was on the right track.

I will continue to point out how damaging relating is in conversations throughout this book. Why will I keep bringing up relating? Because people tell me it's the hardest to understand and it's our worst habit.

I was at a coffee shop a few weeks ago and a woman, about 25 years old, came in. One of her legs was covered in brightly colored tattoos. The tattoos had green vines and colored flowers. It was very beautiful. The other leg didn't have any tattoos at all. She sat near me, so I said, "Your tattoo is beautiful, tell me about it."

She said, "I was very young when I got pregnant. I had to make a decision about my pregnancy. I chose life for my baby and now he is the joy of my life. I don't know what I'd do without him. The tattoo is all about that decision. One leg colorful. One plain."

I could hardly speak. I said, "Wow! Thank you for sharing that. I am deeply moved by your story,"

She smiled and said, "Thank you. I finished high school a few years ago and now I am going to college. I'm a little behind schedule. But it's all worth it because I have my child. We're a family."

As I wiped away a tear of joy I said, "I just want to acknowledge you for making a bold statement about your love for your child. I am blessed because of your story."

There was a time in my life when I would have thought how strange it was to have one leg covered in so many tattoos that you couldn't see any skin, and the other leg plain. I didn't realize how judgmental I was. And because I was so judgmental, I missed so much joy and connection in my life. My challenge to you is to take a look at your life and see if there's something you're judging that's robbing you of peace and joy.

After conducting one of my education seminars, a middle aged man, Larry, came up to me and said, "I am a supervisor and I have to give my advice to people. I have to judge them. It's my job to give my opinion."

I asked, "How's that working for you?"

Larry hesitated and then he said, "Honestly, not very well."

I asked, "Does your team feel judged?"

Larry said, "Probably."

I asked, "Permission to give advice?"

He said, "Yes."

I said, "I suggest you try the Reeves Connection Method. Create each member of your team as extraordinary, create the moment as important. Search for their virtues and values. Listen and lead the conversation. Acknowledge your team for the virtues and values you see in them. Don't relate. Don't give opinions or advice. Don't judge. Instead, ask them about their job and what they like best about it."

I said, "Then tell them you have a request. Whatever you want them to do, put it in the form of a request. Such as, I have a request. I need this completed by Friday at 2pm. Ask them if they have any questions? Then ask them to push back."

Larry said, "What do you mean push back?"

I said, "You know, they probably have an opinion about what you just asked them to do. Right?"

He said, "Yes."

I asked, "Would you rather know their opinion or have them keep it to themselves?"

He said, "I would rather know it."

I said, "Then, ask them about it. Say something like, 'Do you have any other thoughts about this? Is there a better way that you'd like to do this?' If they say no, then you can say, 'Well, we are in agreement then. Thank you.' Get all their feedback out in the open."

I continued, "If they have a better idea, then you just learned something from them. Ask them about it and discuss it with them. Think of your position as more like a coach. Many times, teams win because they want to win for their coach. If they know you respect them, they will want to win for you."

Larry said, "Wow! I get it. I never ask them for their ideas. I thought it was my job to tell them what to do. I see where my problem is. This is great stuff!"

I added, "If you have a great discussion with them, acknowledge them for being a great team and thank them for their open and candid feedback. Make sure they always know that you have a desire to hear their ideas."

Larry said, "My turnover is high. Many times I lose my best people. I am sure this is going help."

People who are invested in something want to feel part of a decision that affects them. If I can make people want to confess to a crime they committed, surely we can make employees want to complete our requests!

As leaders, we have to learn to inspire our teams with something other than the 'fear of our anger.' For example, if a team has frustrated us by not completing a project or display correctly, would they be motivated by threats? I don't believe teams are inspired by hearing their boss say, "Tell me why I shouldn't be angry about this!" Fear may have a short term motivational effect. But it comes at the cost of losing your team members' hearts and minds.

People want to follow a leader because a leader leads. We can deal with behavior we don't like and still see the team member as extraordinary. Instead of thinking about what's wrong, let's go out and inspire people to greatness.

In summary: If you want to connect with people, don't relate. Don't give your opinions or your advice to anyone. And don't judge people. If we stopped doing these three things, how much time would that free up? No relating. No opinions or advice. And no judging. Now that we have all this space freed up in our lives, we have room for the five-step-process to inspire people to greatness.

Dale Reeves

How to Connect

The Five Steps

The next five chapters explain the five steps of how to connect using the Reeves Connection Method. These five steps are all about creation. This is not positive thinking. I don't have any clever quotes for you to memorize. I don't have any jokes to make you laugh or to put you in a positive mood. Our brains like to make assumptions and associations. Some people have said, "Oh, this is like positive thinking." Beware of taking shortcuts to understanding this powerful method!

The Reeves Connection Method doesn't teach you how to think positively. I tell people that this is *not at all* like positive thinking! This connection method is about creation. You will simply take the moment and create something.

We can agree that each of us can create things. Some of us can create a picture on a piece of paper or a sculpture out of clay. We can create a story or a bird house. In the

Reeves Connection Method you are going to create understanding.

We usually don't think about creating a situation or creating a conversation. But that is exactly what you are going to learn to do in this book. You are going to create an extraordinary moment. You are going to create a conversation using a step-by-step method. You are actually going to create greatness in the other person. In return, you will create greatness in yourself.

Right now, if you wanted to, you could create a smile in someone else. You could say something that would cause another person to smile. You can create joy in other people's lives. And you can create joy and success in your own life.

In explaining the Reeves Connection Method I could give you the 50-step process necessary to inspire people to greatness. I could tell you how to sit up in your chair and how to have the right tone in your voice. I could teach you to open your eyes to make sure you aren't squinting. I could tell you to smile. However, you already do those things when you think someone is extraordinary. When you do the five steps of the Reeves Connection Method, you will *naturally* do all fifty steps of the process. You will be doing them instinctively.

Step one is to create the person you are with as extraordinary. When you are with an extraordinary person, you will automatically show a deep interest in them. It's exciting to be with an extraordinary person.

Step two is to create this present moment as very important. When you create this moment as important, it causes you to ask the right questions. I don't need to give you a list of questions to ask in each and every circumstance. When you are with an extraordinary person and it is a very important moment, you automatically ask the right questions. You sincerely want to know more about the other person.

In step three, when you search for virtues and values, this will teach you what to listen for. You don't need a multi-step process in order to find someone's virtues and values. We simply find what we are searching for. In step three you are listening for the virtues and values that lay behind what the other person is saying. When you actually see virtues and values behind the words someone is speaking, you will see something you admire about them.

In step four, when you listen to someone and lead the conversation, you are putting the emphasis on allowing the other person to look good. You provide the framework so they can shine.

In step five, because you are inspired by their virtues and values, you simply thank them for the positive impact they've had on you.

This is your creation. The steps flow naturally because you create them. As you work through each step of the five step process, you create a connection with another person. Your connection with this person will be genuine because you see their virtues and values. You find significance in who they are. They become extraordinary right before your eyes. The other person feels that someone recognizes who they are and sees the best in them. This enlivens them and inspires them to greatness. Their confidence grows as they recognize the potential and ability they possess. They recognize that they have something to give to the world.

I feel as though I need to explain what I mean by creating an extraordinary moment. This is not about being creative in an artsy sense. It's not about creating exquisite sculptures or beautiful landscapes. It's not about creating a mood. It's not about lighting candles and putting out wine glasses. It's not about these connotations of being creative at all.

When creating a moment, you are acting in a dominant and leading mode. You are in charge, but you are listening. You actually take the moment you have, and you create something powerful and extraordinary out of your moment. You make a choice to create this moment into something special. It starts with a declaration.

As an interrogator, I am in charge of the conversation. I take control. However, I direct the conversation so the person I'm interrogating does most of the talking. I create the moment into what I want it to be.

As I said earlier, I'm not listening to people so I can resonate to them on their level. Instead, I am listening to them so I can bring them toward my thoughts. I'm connecting to them on my level, not on their level. Remember, it's my goal to inspire them. I am creating this moment.

On career personality tests I don't score high in the creative category, but I do score high in dominance.

I grew up on a dairy farm. Farm kids have to be resourceful. I realized I could have the kind of day I wanted by creating it, but I had to be dominant and I had to choose to create it.

I hated chores. But living on a farm, I had to help my dad in his business of farming. Chores were done seven days a week, two to four hours in the morning and four hours each evening. When I was home from school, there were eight to ten hours of extra farm work that needed to be done in-between the chores every day. After my list of work was done, I may have had some time to play.

I created each of my chores as a game. Milking cows twice a day seven days a week is not an easy job. The cows stink. You have to clean them, feed them and clean up after them. I simply took control of my thoughts and created farm work as a game. I made it fun. I was driving the truck on our farm when I was in 5th grade.

When I was seven-years-old I did experiments testing the memory of the baby geese on our farm. I placed food at the end of a maze that I made out of cardboard boxes. I cut flaps in the cardboard which they pushed open to follow the trail of grain. I would change the pattern of the maze and watch the geese become confused at first, but quickly learn the new path. The geese and I entertained ourselves in this way when I had a few minutes of free time. At mealtime, I would eat quickly and then run outside and play with the geese before my dad was finished with his meal. When my dad was finished eating, it was time to get back to work.

Thinking back, I have always created my day. I usually find a company I want to work for and I walk in the front door and ask to speak to the person in charge. I don't wait for a job posting.

I have only applied for one job from an advertisement. I went to that job interview because I wanted to practice interviewing. A new hotel was being built in town, and I decided that I wanted to manage the restaurant in the hotel when it was built. I thought if I interviewed for management jobs once a month, I'd be ready to interview for the job I really wanted in two years when the hotel was finished. I planned that this would give me 24 practice interviews.

I went on my first practice interview. I interviewed for a management job with a restaurant owner. The restaurant owner told me he was interviewing 30 people for this position. I thought my interview went pretty well. I got called back for a second interview and he offered me the position.

I told him, "I really don't want this job. This was just a practice interview for me."

I went on to tell him my story. He told me he liked my confidence and communication skills. He said he really wanted to hire me for this position and he offered me a good salary. I took the job he offered me as a restaurant manager. Thinking back, I completed my goal of being a restaurant manager 24 months ahead of schedule (just at a different restaurant.)

I realize that the seeds of this technique of creation came naturally for me. Connection and creation was also how I got my job as a police officer.

I was 18 years old. I heard about a part time police job opening in the neighboring city. I drove to the city, stopped at the first house I saw, and knocked on the door. Someone came to the door. I said, "Hi. Where does the mayor live?" They told me how to get to the mayor's house.

I drove to the mayor's house, knocked on the door and said, "I heard you have a police officer job opening. I'd like that job!"

The mayor seemed doubtful, "I've never had anyone come to my door to apply for a job before."

I asked, "Well, what do you need to know?" We talked for a while and connected.

After a few minutes he said, "Well, all right. You got the job. Report to the police chief."

I asked, "Where does the Chief of Police live?"

The mayor told me where the Police Chief lived and said, "I'll call him and tell him you're on your way."

I drove to the Chief's house, knocked on the door and said, "Hello! I'm your new officer!"

He said, "So I hear."

I started my police officer training the next day.

I created getting the job. I was dominant and I did not wait around for others to apply. The moment I heard about the job opening, I created getting that job. I created the moment as very important, so I did what was very important to achieving my goal. When I created the moment as very important, it was easy to know what to do next. I drove to the town, and asked where the mayor lived.

I've learned that either I create my day or I am the victim of my day. Better said, I either choose to create my day or I choose to be a victim of my day.

Since realizing this, I've made the habit of waking up every day and saying I choose to create this day as the best day I've ever had. I say to myself, "I create this day as the best day I've ever had."

At first I thought this was silly. How could each day be better than the one before? However, that's exactly what happened. Every day *was* better. And then it dawned on

me. Of course every day was better than the day before.
Because, I would rather actually be alive and live any day
than just have the remembrance of a good day. Living is
much better than remembering. Life actually lived is
amazing!

If I thought that the best day of my life was one already in
the past, then what would that mean for today?

Is there any virtue in defending the memory of a day as
being 'the best I ever had' and sabotaging today so it can't
possibly be as good as the one day I call the best? I guess I
could create this day to be the second best day I ever had.
However, that doesn't inspire me to greatness.

We don't live in the past, we live in the present. Or maybe
some of us think we do live in the past. Maybe that's our
problem; we are still trying to live in the past. That is an
impossible effort. I am alive *now*. I am not alive in the past.
The past is a memory.

Someone said, "But what if yesterday you won a billion
dollars in the lottery? How could today be better than that
day?" I said, "I guess, because I'd be spending the money
and that's better than winning it."

My father has lost his short term memory. Every day is new
for him. Better said, every moment is new for him. I

remember one night he choked on a piece of hard candy. He couldn't breathe. The hard candy was lodged in his wind pipe. He was turning blue. My wife and I pulled him up from his chair and she did the Heimlich maneuver on him. The candy flew out of his mouth. She saved his life!

As we sat there full of adrenalin for a few minutes, he said, "Who's turn is it to deal the cards?"

I said, "You almost died! You had candy stuck in your wind pipe."

He said, "No I didn't. Let's play cards."

He was calm and we were nervous. He didn't remember anything about it. He wasn't worried at all. It made me think. Maybe he enjoys life more than we do. He's not stuck on what just happened. He lives life now. He is only in the moment that is here.

Why would I ever take a chance on having a bad day? And why would I label a day as bad when only a few things went wrong. If I expect everyone to be nice to me and if I expect everything to go my way, I would have to say that I have unrealistic expectations.

If someone stole 60 dollars from you, would you spend 86,400 dollars trying to get the 60 dollars back? That wouldn't be a wise business practice! What if someone stole 3,600 dollars from you? Would you spend 86,400 dollars trying to get the 3,600 dollars back? Of course you wouldn't. That would be considered foolish.

So if someone steals 60 seconds of our time by yelling at us, why would we spend the rest of the day complaining about it and thinking about how unfair that person was to us?

There are 86,400 seconds in a day. Sometimes we even have a hard time going to sleep just thinking about how unfair someone was to us. If someone wastes an hour of our time, 3,600 seconds, why waste 86,400 seconds fretting and complaining about it?

Sometimes we struggle to be who we really are because we get so caught up and upset about how someone else has treated us. If we get upset because of what someone else said to us, we are being controlled by something outside of ourselves. We can easily become victims of other people's words. But we can break out of victimhood by simply creating an extraordinary moment.

Possibly, we get attention by complaining about other people. Complaining usually helps us relate to other complainers. Maybe we feel part of something when we complain with others. We get to complain about being a victim of some sort of circumstance. We get to tell others how bad it is to endure whatever it is we feel we have to endure.

It's pretty easy to complain. We've been doing that since we've been toddlers. And if that's how you want to live, it's okay. I would, however, encourage you to choose to create your day. Even though bad things happen in life, you don't have to be controlled by outside forces. You can choose to create something new!

Maybe we should try creating a connection with someone we feel we have to tolerate. If you can forgive and forget the past, you can live today and create something special for today. Your life will be better.

Some of us have complained for days and even years about something that happened to us one day in the past. We waste millions of seconds of our lives fretting about something someone said to us or did to us. I've learned that I need to give these moments up, because they are in the past. They have nothing to do with my present day.

If we want to waste something, we should waste money instead of time. We only get 24 hours a day. It's impossible to get more time, so don't waste it by complaining and feeling upset. You can get more money, but you can't get more time. It's impossible.

I often hear one person ask another, "How are you?"

The other person responds, "I'm okay so far, but it's early. Things could change."

Sometimes we set ourselves up to fail. It's almost as if some of us are looking for that one thing that could ruin our day. If that's what we are looking for, it won't be hard to find.

Rather than being dragged down by this unintentional world view, I have chosen that I am not the victim of other people's opinions. I'm not even the victim of my own judgments. I'm not the victim of how my day goes. I choose to create my day. I choose to create each day as the best day I've ever had! I choose to create connection. Let's learn how to do that next.

Step One: Extraordinary

(How to Connect)

Create others as extraordinary.

Create people as extraordinary before you see any *evidence* that they are extraordinary.

We do this with a newborn baby. We see them for the first time and we think they are *so* extraordinary! The first few weeks at home, we look into their eyes with wonder and amazement. But if we looked for evidence, really, all they do is cry and poop their pants.

Then, later in life when they don't cry or poop their pants anymore, we say to them, "What's the matter with you boy? You got a C in math?!"

Innately, we know how to create people as extraordinary. We do it with newborn babies. And it's wonderful. I love babies. They are true miracles.

Try this:
When you see someone, whether you already know them

or not, say to yourself, "This person is extraordinary!" Create them as extraordinary without any evidence. We create people as extraordinary all the time, under certain circumstances.

Let me explain with an example.

Let's imagine that you have a project due at 1 pm, but you are very hungry. Not only is this project due at 1 pm, but you need to present it to your boss at 1 pm. You don't want to be hungry during the meeting, so you pick up your lap-top and go to a restaurant to grab a quick lunch.

Luckily for you, there are a few tables available at this restaurant. You grab a table that has two chairs and you order your lunch.

As you are sitting at this restaurant someone comes up to you and asks, "Is this seat taken? Would it be okay if I sit here?"

Because you feel hurried, you might let them know that it would be okay, but you would give the person some body language that tells them, "Don't bother me." You stare at your computer and don't make eye contact with the other person as you say something like, "I suppose it would be okay."

Would your response be different if the person asking to share your table was your favorite movie actor or actress? What if they just happened to be in town for a movie shoot and they were hungry and needed a quick bite. Most of us would close the computer and say, "Of course, please sit down. What are you doing in town? I've always wanted to meet you."

Consider that your response might be different if the person who asked to sit at your table was one of your favorite celebrities. What if it was your favorite sports player or coach?

I know I would close my computer and think to myself, "The whole office will understand if my report isn't done because I had lunch with, _____? (Fill in the blank with your favorite actor, actress or other celebrity.) We know the whole office will understand, because obviously, this person is extraordinary!

We probably wouldn't relate to the celebrity. We would listen and lead. We'd ask them questions such as, "What was your favorite movie to act in and why?" We would see them as extraordinary.

Our minds would tell us things like, "They were on Mars!"

"They saved the world!"

"They won the World Championship!"

"Of course they are extraordinary!"

You already know how to create someone as extraordinary. You don't need to be told how to do it. You don't need a 50-step process to make sure you create someone as extraordinary. If your favorite celebrity showed up at your lunch table, you would automatically do all the right things that would make the celebrity feel extraordinary in your presence. You wouldn't even have to try because you'd be so excited.

Consider the fact that most of the actors and actresses we love are people we've never seen in real life. We've only watched them act. They make their living by pretending to be someone else, and it's actually the-someone-else that we've seen and consider extraordinary. (I'm not at all inferring that actors and actresses don't work hard, or that they aren't extraordinary individuals in their own right. Obviously they have worked hard to get to where they are.)

For this example, consider that we know very little about who our favorite celebrity really is. We create them in our minds and behavior as someone extraordinary. Think about sitting there, at lunch, with your favorite celebrity. This is what it can feel like if you create people as extraordinary before you have evidence that they are extraordinary.

The first thing I say to myself when I meet someone is, "This is an extraordinary person!" I see the person as amazing and extraordinary. I don't see them as just ordinary.

Because I create people around me as extraordinary, I am surrounded by extraordinary people. I used to be surrounded by ordinary people because I saw them as just ordinary. (Unless, of course, they did something super-amazing and I had evidence that they were extraordinary.)

I usually get a few strange looks from the people in my audiences as I introduce the subject of creating other people as extraordinary. That's okay. Most of us are used to taking each day as it comes, and haven't even considered doing this. But after I speak on this subject for a few minutes, the people in my seminars begin to brighten up with understanding as they see the simplicity and power of creating people as extraordinary.

If you create people as extraordinary, they will show up as extraordinary.

Let me share a story.

I was called to do an investigation into a situation where a female had stolen quite a few things from a retail store. A week before I got to the store, the owner and a consultant had talked to this woman for over an hour. She had denied taking anything during their entire conversation.

I arrived at the store a week later. Usually after the suspect has denied any accusations of theft at the first questioning session, it is difficult to get a confession a week later. Almost immediately after I arrived at the store, the suspect, a 35 year old woman, walked into the office. She was extremely early and I had not taken the time I usually take to prepare for an interview and interrogation.

I always take a few minutes to create the other person as extraordinary, and work myself through the five steps of connection before every interview and interrogation. However, on this occasion, I didn't have time to go through these simple steps.

I asked the woman to sit down and we started talking. The interrogation was not going very well. Forty five minutes into our conversation I realized that I had not yet created this woman as extraordinary. So while she was talking, without changing my facial expression, I told myself, "This is an extraordinary person sitting before me." Even though I consciously did not change my facial expression, and even though she was looking down at the floor at the time, she stopped for about ten seconds in mid-sentence. She looked up and smiled at me. Then she continued talking. About five minutes later she confessed to over thirty times more theft than we knew about.

It was then that I realized people can tell when someone else thinks they are extraordinary. I mean, don't you know when someone thinks you are extraordinary? We can tell if another person thinks we are amazing and extraordinary. We can also tell if someone doesn't like us at all. We can tell.

It was that day that I realized there actually is another realm of communication that is above verbal and body language. With the hope of not sounding too bizarre, I have come to realize that people really can connect on a different level if you create it.

Think about someone special that you think is extraordinary. It should be somebody that is in your everyday life. Maybe it's a friend, a child or a spouse. Sometimes you know what they are feeling even before they say anything. We may think this is because we have known this special person for a long time. But, consider for a moment, it may possibly be because you created this person as being extraordinary. And now you have a deeper language and understanding with this friend.

Have you ever had the experience of knowing someone is in trouble and calling them at the exact right time? I'm not talking about a feeling. You may describe it as a feeling, but it's actually communication on a deeper level.

My sister, Donna Jean, had a dog that she loved. My mom and dad said that she played with that dog every day. Nonetheless, on the farm, they could not keep every dog that was born, so they gave him to a farmer that lived about seven miles away.

When my sister, Donna Jean, was five years old she died from Spinal Meningitis. She was in the ambulance on the way to the hospital when she died. In our small community, people listened to the radio every day to hear the obituaries. That's how they found out if a neighbor was suffering and needed some help.

The farmer who now owned the dog, came to my parents' house the next day. He told my parents that the dog, who used to play with Donna Jean, had howled and cried all night long, starting at about midnight. He could not make the dog settle down. The farmer told them that the dog had never howled at night before. The farmer heard about my sister's death on the radio the next morning and he said it was obvious to him that the dog somehow knew that Donna Jean had died, even though they were miles apart. He asked my parents, "What time of day did Donna Jean die yesterday?" My dad said, "Right before midnight."

Consider for a moment, there is a language that is deeper than words can express. And **you** can tap into that language by creating people as extraordinary.

I understand that this example is about a dog and a little girl, instead of between two people. But maybe the dog was less distracted than most people are, and the dog was listening and paying attention to this deep communication.

We have two ways to consider whether someone is extraordinary. One way is to wait and see if the person is extraordinary. The 'show-me-first' way. 'I will judge if you are extraordinary or not based on my knowledge and my experiences. I will form an opinion about it after I see the evidence and I then I will make a judgement.' The 'show-me-first' way is about opinions and judging.

On the other hand, you can create a person as extraordinary without any evidence. Creating a person as extraordinary frees you up from constantly judging them!

When you create your colleagues, neighbors and the people you meet as extraordinary it will only take a few seconds of your time. However, when you create someone as extraordinary, it will enrich your life and the lives of those around you.

Connection was the sole reason I was successful in sales. In the late 1990s I was a salesman selling food to restaurants. We had over 75 salespeople in the company. The company gave me a territory and enough established accounts to keep me busy. Nonetheless, in my first year, I had more new accounts than anyone else. I didn't relate to people, I connected with them. The customers trusted me and I opened new accounts with ease.

We had a sales event. The person who sold the most restaurant equipment won a trip to Napa Valley. I enjoyed the free trip to Napa Valley. It was wonderful.

I won the event by connecting to the owners and the staff of the restaurants I served. I saw them as extraordinary people. I saw them as powerful people and I treated them as though they had extraordinary lives.

Do you want to be surrounded by extraordinary people? Create people as extraordinary. This is step one. Try it. You've got nothing to lose and everything to gain.

Creating people as extraordinary is a fairly straight-forward thing to do. It takes practice. I suggest you start this habit immediately. Think of a few people in your life and create them as extraordinary right now. You'll be amazed at the difference it will make.

Dale Reeves

Step Two: Very Important Moment

(How to Connect)

Create this moment as a very important moment.

Create this moment as a very significant moment in your life. Tell yourself, "I create this moment as very important."

There is a big difference between considering and creating.

If you create a moment as special, you create the moment *before* it happens. You are in charge of the moment the second you create it. The moment becomes important and you will take action immediately. You are a participant in the moment. During an important moment, people move into action.

If you saw a car accident happen, you'd take immediate action because the moment is very important. Some of us would run to the cars and try to help. Others would call 911 immediately. What if at the accident, one of the car doors opened and a dazed child stepped into the street with traffic approaching? We would all take immediate action. We know how to take action at an important moment when we feel urgency.

But most of us don't feel urgency for the moments of our everyday lives. We'll move into action to save someone's life. We'll move into action to escape a tiger, in order to save our own lives. But for some reason, we usually only respond when something other than ourselves creates the moment as important.

My challenge to you is to see each moment in your life as important. We only have a limited number of moments in our lives. Seize the moment and create it as important all on your own, without someone or something else forcing it on you.

Some of us reach a milestone birthday, maybe it's at 30-years-old, 40-years-old, or 60-years-old. And we take a look back at our lives. We may think, "I thought I'd be at a different place in my life at this milestone." We may feel disappointed because we haven't achieved what we thought we might have by this time in our lives. Maybe this is because we didn't create our moments and realize their importance. Maybe it's because we only did what someone or something else forced us to do. We only saw importance in the moment, when we were forced by someone else to see its importance.

Don't consider a moment

The word 'consider' means to think carefully about something before making a decision. When you consider whether a moment is important or not, you are waiting until the moment is over and then you will judge whether the moment *was* important or not. When you consider a moment, you are a spectator.

If you have to think carefully about the moment before creating it, you're too late to be a participant. You are a spectator. Spectators don't make a difference, they just watch. Maybe a spectator cheers from the sidelines, but they don't play in the game.

Participants make a difference in people's lives and in their own lives. You could spend your whole life considering, measuring, and deciding if your last moment was good or bad. By the time you've made your decision, it would be too late.

When I create a moment, I do not think carefully about the moment. I boldly create the moment as very important. I create the moment before it happens. I create it now. The moment is important because I said it was! Period.

In the Reeves Connection Method, we don't consider anything. We create and we take ownership. The Reeves

Connection Method is about creating a conversation. In step one we create the other person as extraordinary. Step two is about creating the moment as very important. When you create the moment as very important, you automatically do what is important. It is a declaration. It's a call to action.

When we create something, we take ownership of our creation.

Why am I suggesting that we create this moment as an important moment?

When we see this moment as very important, we ask the right questions. We give the moment our all and automatically make the most out of it. I don't have to give you a 50-step process to create the moment as important. When you create this moment as very important, you automatically do the right things.

Time does not exist

Additionally, create this moment as a very important moment because ***it's all we have!*** Life only gives us one moment at a time. We live life one moment at a time. We cannot re-live this morning. We cannot say to ourselves, "I'm going to save 7 to 8 am today. I plan to spend 7 to 8 am, later this evening at 6 pm." No. That doesn't work.

Time is the great equalizer. Everyone has a different amount of money, but everyone in the world has 24 hours in a day. Nobody gets 27 hours and nobody gets 21 hours.

You cannot **buy** time. Even a million dollars cannot buy you an extra minute. You might think, "Yes I can. I can hire someone to clean my house and wash my car. Therefore, I am buying time." However, you are not buying time. You are buying efficiency. You're just doing a different activity.

The time is still passing at the same speed it always does. 24 hours from now, it will be tomorrow. It doesn't matter how much money you spend on efficiency today. In seven days it will be next week. Don't confuse efficiency with time.

And here is the big lie we have bought for years. We act as though time really exists. We think we can *save* time. We think we can *manage* time. But in reality, time does not exist in that way.

Our concept of time exists, like a tape measure exists. We can measure time. We can set the timer on the microwave to go off in 30 minutes. We can set an alarm to go off at 8 am. We can measure that the Cubs haven't won the World Series in 108 years. But we can't go back in time and change that to 107 years. Now, we can say, "They won the World Series in 2016."

The invention of watches and clocks must have been earth-shattering for people. To be able to take something with you that can measure time as it's passing, must have been incredible for the people of those days. Everyone's watch is measuring time. Knowing the time of day is now fundamental knowledge. But that's what a watch does, it measures time. It cannot manage time. It cannot save time.

A man once told me, "What do you mean you can't manage time? I've been to time management seminars."

I asked, "And how's that 'time management' working for you?"

He said, "Not very well."

"You can manage activity, but you can't manage time. Can you manage an hour and change it into 55 minutes?" I asked.

He said, "No."

I said, "But you can manage your activity right?"

He responded, "Okay. That makes sense."

I said, "And, you can manage your thoughts. You can manage how much you value each moment, right?"

He said, "I agree with that. But *each moment* isn't really important is it? I mean most of my day is just ordinary."

"That's simply because you choose to see your day as ordinary. Therefore, you may be missing many important things along the way," I told him. "It's your choice if you see each breath as precious or each human being as ordinary or extraordinary."

"Okay, that makes sense. That's helpful. Thank you for your explanation," he said.

I choose to make each moment important. Each breath is precious and each human being is a beautiful creation! When I choose to make each day important and each moment important, it changes my whole day.

Scientists will say that time does exist. Time does exist as a scientific measurement. But in the world of life and management, time does not exist as we think it does. One year from now you will be a year older. There is nothing you can do about it. You can try to hide from time in a cave or fill your year with constant activity. Nonetheless, whatever you choose to do, you will still be a year older, one year from now.

We can try to look as though we aren't aging. We can use procedures to hide our wrinkles, and transplant hair back on our heads. But we can't stop time from passing. We will still be one year older, one year from now.

Time only exists as a measurement. We can measure it backward. We try to measure it forward, by making plans. However, we can't spend it forward or backward. We can only spend it now.

So why is this moment a very important moment? Because, it's all you have! This moment **right now** is *all* you have!

It's all we *ever* have!

Consider a minute. It doesn't matter if you want to spend it or not. It is spent. It cannot be saved. You can hire someone to do your laundry, but it doesn't give you more time. You will just spend that time doing something other than laundry. That moment in time will be automatically spent. You cannot stop time from happening.

In fact, you actually don't spend time. Time spends you. No matter what you are doing in this moment, you and I are in the same moment. Time is spending us.

Every minute, every one of us gets one minute older. Time spends us. There is nothing you can do about it. Time will spend you and me equally.

It took me two years to get my head around this concept. But once I embraced it, it helped slow my world down. No. I didn't get more time, but the time seemed to pass more slowly. My days became more beautiful because I was present to the moments of my day. I enjoy the conversations I have because I know each moment is precious.

Let me tell you a story.

I was at a conference, volunteering. I showed up early and asked the conference manager if they needed anything done. The woman in charge of the conference said the glass on the front door needed to be cleaned. I told her I would take care of it.

As I walked up to the glass door I noticed a woman sitting on the couch in the entryway. I had never seen the women before this moment. I said to myself, "This woman is extraordinary and this is a very important moment."

I didn't say, "How are you?" I simply said, "Good morning. What do you do?"

She said, "I'm a grade school teacher."

I asked, "What grade do you teach?"

She responded, "Third grade."

I asked, "What do you like best about third grade?"

She said, "I don't know. I've never thought about it."

As I was spraying the front door with glass cleaner and wiping the glass with a paper towel I said, "I've got time to listen."

After about thirty seconds she told me, "I don't know. I guess the reason I like third grade is because the children are old enough to learn some complicated things. But they aren't too old to give me a hug and tell me that they love me. And I can hug them back and tell them that I love them." She hesitated for a moment and then asked me, "Is that bad?"

I replied, "No. That's not bad. In fact, it's incredible! I wish you had been my third grade teacher. I want to acknowledge you for loving those children. You're an amazing teacher!"

She stood up with a panicked look on her face and said, "I'm about to make the mistake of my life! I just called my principle last night and told her I want to take the opening and move to sixth grade. I've got to make a phone call right now!"

She pulled out her cell phone and ran off down the hall. I finished cleaning the door. About ten minutes later she came up to me and gave me a big hug.

She said, "Thank you for saving my life! I called my principle and he is allowing me to stay in third grade. You helped me see what was important to me in life."

So I ask you, the reader, what did I do to save her life? All I did was to create her as extraordinary and create the moment as important. When you create people as extraordinary and when you create the moment as a very important moment, all the important things fall into place.

Now she knows what she loves in life, and why she loves it. She instantly saw the moment as very important and she took immediate action. She was inspired to greatness. Because of our conversation, she recognized the value she brought to the world through her work with children.

I was also inspired. I had the experience of making a difference in this teacher's life by helping her see how extraordinary she was. She went back to caring for those little third graders. I could imagine their happy faces as they were taught by a teacher who loved them and realized the importance of the work she was doing.

That's why I'm writing this book. If we just take a moment to inspire people to greatness, there's no telling what they'll realize about themselves and the difference it will make in the world. This moment, right now, is very important!

It doesn't take very long to inspire people to greatness. In the short conversation I just told you, I went through the five steps to the Reeves Connection Method. I created the woman as extraordinary and the moment as very important. I also listened for her virtues and values. I listened and led. And I acknowledged her. We will learn about those three steps in the next chapters.

This is important: I did not relate. I did not give an opinion. And I did not judge her.

I could have related and said, "Oh, my cousin is a third grade teacher and she is always talking about those basic skills tests." Or I could have told her about some traumatic experience I had in third grade. When trying to relate there is always a lot to choose from. However, that would have made it all about me and what I knew about third grade.

I could have given an opinion and said, "I don't know how you do it! I doubt I could teach a classroom full of small children. I'm not good at that kind of thing." But again, that would have made it all about me.

Or I could have just said the usual, "How are you?" But that would have been so ordinary. When we create the moment as very important, we don't treat our moment as ordinary.

I simply said, "Good morning. What do you do?" I showed interest in her.

Why did I show interest in her? It is easy to show interest in someone who is extraordinary. Wouldn't you want to know what an extraordinary person does?

If you and I were sitting at a table in a restaurant and I said to you, "Look at that woman over there, she is an extraordinary person!" It would be natural for you to ask, "What does she do?"

Every one of us would want to meet an extraordinary person. Once you create someone as an extraordinary person, your whole thought process changes.

By creating the moment as a very important moment, I am not afraid to ask a question. I know this is a very important moment, and I don't want to waste it.

The third grade teacher told me I saved her life, and I did it while cleaning glass on a door. I didn't have to go to a homeless shelter to make a difference in someone's life. I made a difference in her life while doing an ordinary task, simply by creating the moment as very important.

Don't get me wrong. Volunteering at a homeless shelter is an awesome and important thing to do. I'm just asking you to consider that right now, wherever you are, you can inspire people to greatness. You can make a difference in people's lives right now. Anyplace. Anytime.

Our days are full of moments we waste. We waste them by thinking of something else. Did you ever drive to work and not remember your drive because you were thinking about something else? Most of us have. How safe is that? What did we solve by thinking of something else? How many of us spend our days on autopilot while we are preoccupied with our thoughts?

Have you ever been listening to someone, only to have your mind wander off on another topic? Then you had to say, "I'm sorry, could you repeat that?" If you had created the moment as very important, you probably would have paid attention, because it was a very important moment.

How would you listen if your boss said to you? "Come over here and sit down. What I'm going to say to you is very important." I'm sure we'd listen undistracted to this conversation. Why does someone else have to tell us something is very important, before we listen intently?

If we value life and other human beings, isn't the moment always important when another person is sharing something with us?

How much time goes by while we are preoccupied? Days? Weeks? Years? How many of our moments do we miss because we are thinking or worrying about other things?

If we want to be present to the moment, we can't just let our brains run on their own. Our brains are wired for survival. If you or I allow our brain to run its own course it will take the path of least resistance and it will focus on surviving. Survival is not a bad way to live, but it's rather boring and safe. Survival isn't very exciting or extraordinary.

I don't know many people who want their gravestone to read, "He played it safe and survived a bit longer than most."

Or, "He worried a lot because he wanted to always be safe, thus he died early."

This reminds me of a quote credited to Mark Twain: "I am an old man and have known a great many troubles, but most of them never happened."

Successful people do not take the path of least resistance. I was in a meeting years ago and somebody said to the CEO, "If we build the new store exactly as you're suggesting, we could be sued."

The CEO replied, "If I was worried about being sued, I wouldn't open the front door. Now, let's talk about how we can make this work."

You have to stop letting your brain grind away over one imaginary worry after another in its attempt to make sure you survive. Our species wants to survive. Our brains are wired to survive. Give your brain the choice and it will choose to focus on surviving.

To avoid spending your whole life trying to survive you must create something. You have to take control of your thoughts. Taking control of your thoughts is an assertive action. You must create your moments as important, or stand by as your brain lets the moments waste away.

I feel as though I need to explain the difference between creating the moment as important, and using positive thinking. Taking control of my thoughts may sound like I'm using positively thinking. But creating the moment as important is completely different than positive thinking.

Positive thinking has helped a lot of people get away from their negative thoughts about themselves or others. I feel as though positive thinking has its place in the world.

However, I do not conduct an interrogation using positive thinking. I don't say to myself, "I am going to think positively about this moment, therefore I will be successful and I will get a confession."

When I conduct an interrogation I'm not focused on my own success. I am focused on being accurate. I desire to get to the truth. I will be having an intense conversation with another person during the interrogation. I take this very seriously.

The Reeves Connection Method causes a connection between two people. Creating the moment as very important causes me to pay attention to what is there. This takes away the distractions and therefore causes me to be focused on the present moment.

I'd like to share a story that helps explain the difference between the Reeves Connection Method and positive thinking.

I was having a conversation with a friend of mine and he asked, "How is creating the moment any different than positive thinking?"

I said to him, "Please define positive thinking for me." (A good interrogator always asks the other person to define a key word or phrase.)

He said, "Well, positive thinking means I focus on the positive side of life. I expect I will be successful. I will have good health and happiness. I know everything is going to work out for the best in my life."

I responded, "I admire your positive outlook toward your success."

He said, "Thank you. I say to myself that people are going to see me on top of the mountain or dead at the bottom."

I responded, "Wow! You are so committed to your success that you are willing to die for it?"

He said, "Well, okay. Maybe I'm not really willing to *die* for it."

I said, "You just told me you were willing to die for it. Was that a lie? Are you willing to be dead at the bottom or not?"

He quickly responded, "That's just a figure of speech to remind me to try harder."

I said, "I'm sorry, I don't mean to point out anything wrong with your thinking. I truly was admiring your commitment to success. But do you see how your definition of positive thinking makes it all about you? You are thinking positively about things working out for *you* and about the results *you* will get."

I continued, "According to the definition you gave me, positive thinking is all about *your* happiness, *your* results, *your* wealth and *your* health. It sounds a little too self-absorbed and self-focused. Where do other people fit into this? Not that I'm against personal success. If I approached a conversation only thinking about my success and my wealth, I wouldn't be very successful as an interrogator or as a communicator."

He said, "Please explain the difference. I'm not sure I understand."

This is the explanation I gave him:

Positive thinking is like relating in some ways. Remember, do-not-relate is the first habit we need to get rid of because relating is all about 'me'.

When I conduct an interrogation, I get the other person to open up and tell me something they don't want to tell me. Telling them to think positively and that everything is going to work out, would be lying to them. Going to jail doesn't feel like a very positive experience. I desire to treat other people with honesty and integrity.

I don't see any honesty and integrity in saying 'You will see me on top of the mountain or dead on the bottom,' and then saying 'I really don't mean it.'

Positive thinking can be helpful for people who have a tendency to think negative thoughts. Of course, thinking positive thoughts is always better than thinking negative thoughts. I am sure positive thinking has its benefits. It's not my intention to criticize positive thinking.

When I get a confession, I don't do it to get a result in my life. I don't put a notch in my belt when I get a confession. I usually see people to go jail. Sometimes it feels like I just saw a train wreck.

After an interrogation I get satisfaction out of knowing I respected the other person and I left them with their dignity. I get satisfaction from realizing that I inspired them to greatness. I feel my job may resemble the job of an ambulance driver. The driver sees a lot of disaster, and he rarely sees the person restored to full health. But the ambulance driver can take satisfaction in the fact that he is helping people.

Many times the reason people steal something is because they are consumed by thoughts of needing to look successful. They think they need to 'keep up with the Joneses.' They feel they need to be happy and they think that having more money will give them happiness.

The Reeves Connection Method inspires people to see that they can make a difference in other people lives, instead of only thinking about their own personal success.

In The Reeves Connection Method I create the *other* person as extraordinary. I create the moment as very important. I search for the *other* person's virtues and values and I listen and lead the *other* person. I thank them for the difference they made in my life. It's not a gimmick. It's not a game. It's all about the *other* person.

The funny thing is, when I create the people around me as extraordinary, I take for granted that I am extraordinary too. I don't have to prove that I'm extraordinary or look for acceptance. I don't have to psych myself up by saying a lot of positive things about myself. I don't have to prove my self-worth because I see great value and worth all around me in others. I don't even think about myself or what is going to work out for me. Even though I am not thinking about myself or focused on my success, the Reeves Connection Method has given me greater success in every area of my life. And it does this easily and naturally, as an unexpected result of the process of connecting with others.

The Reeves Connection Method is about being present to the riches that are around me in other people.

My friend then said, "Wow! That opened my eyes. I see that thinking positively assumes that something is wrong. Therefore, I must think about it positively, before it consumes me. If I must think positively about something, then there must be something wrong to begin with. It's like trying to chase away the darkness with good ideas and thoughts."

I said, "Anyway, the Reeves Connection Method is about creating a conversation between two people. It is not about thinking.

My friend said, "I see the difference. Positive thinking is all about me. The Reeves Connection Method is all about the other person. Thank you. That helps a lot! I'm going to work on helping other people be successful from now on, starting with my children. You were right, this was a very important moment. You helped me understand."

I said, "Thank you. I admire your willingness to have a candid discussion about something you believe in."

Remember, the Reeves Connection Method is not at all like positive thinking.

Stop worrying and create.

When you create the moment as very important your brain will have conversations with you. Your brain will want to know why the moment is very important. Why is it any more important than the last moment?

But who is in charge? You have to assert your will over the conversation in your head. Give your brain a better job to do than just to survive. Give your brain the job of creating the moment as very important.

I remember, years ago, seeing the cover of a magazine. The cover was divided into two pictures of the same man. One picture had the man sitting at his desk with his swim trunks on. The other picture had him sitting on the sand at the beach while wearing his suit and tie. I looked at that picture and said, "That's just like me. While I'm at work, I am worried that I'm not spending enough time with my family. And while I'm taking a day off with my family, I'm worried about what's going on at work." Since my mind was always worried about these concerns, I wasn't fully engaged or focused on any of my present moments.

Now I know how to overcome this problem of worry and fretting! I take a deep breath. I look around me and then I create this moment as an important moment. Life slows down. I see the moment for what it really is: precious, important and urgent. Creating the moment as very important causes me to take immediate action. I get more done because I see this moment as important.

As I pointed out earlier, I wake up every morning and say to myself, "I create this day as the best day I've ever had." That's how I choose it to be. Or sometimes I say, "I choose to create this day as extraordinary. I choose to create this day as very important. This is the best day I've ever had."

My wife said to me one day, "How can every day be better than the day before? I mean, every one of them?"

I said, "Yes. Because I am actually living this day. All other days are only a memory. I'd rather be alive for a day with all of its possibility, rather than just remember a great day."

I continued, "If I make the choice that I'd rather live a day than remember a day, that makes every day the best day ever. Life happens now. Life *only* happens now."

Every moment is now. Every memory is in the past. I don't want to focus on the past. Focusing on the past seems like a waste of time for me. Oh, I love my memories, but there is a whole world out there! Even if I live to be 100, I know life is short. I don't want to spend many of my moments rehashing a memory. I want to experience each moment in the present. I can live my life as ordinary, or I can live it as extraordinary. It's up to me. Most of us default to taking life as it comes. I would rather create life as I want it, instead of just taking it as it comes.

I asked a man, "What do you like best about your job?"

He responded, "Retirement."

I asked, "So you're retired?"

He said, "Nope. I've still got 15 years to go until I can retire. Then I will enjoy life."

I felt compassion for the man. I'm not sure if he just hated his job, or if he was so focused on retirement that he couldn't enjoy anything for the next 15 years.

But in a way, many of us are like that. Have you ever been on vacation in a beautiful place? Do you enjoy the last day as much as the other days?

I was on vacation in Hawaii. We were scheduled to leave Hawaii on Sunday. My daughter woke up on Saturday morning and I noticed a tear in her eyes. I asked, "What's the matter?"

She said, "This is the last day we have in Hawaii."

I said, "That's right, we have 24 more hours to enjoy in paradise."

She said, "I guess you're right. Instead of crying I could be enjoying the last 24 hours."

We went to the lobby of the hotel, had some coffee, and had a lot of fun on our last day.

But my daughter taught me a very good lesson that day. Be present. Enjoy life where you are. Monday should be just as enjoyable as Friday. It's all in our focus.

I struggled with this as a child. I used to be sad on Sunday starting about noon. I spent all Sunday afternoon thinking, "Tomorrow I have to go to school again for five straight days." How silly of me to waste those Sunday afternoons being sad, when I still had 9 hours left of the weekend to enjoy.

My wedding day was great, but so was the day after, and the day after that. When my children were born, those were amazing days. But so were the days that followed. All of those days are in the past.

I don't grade each day. Let's see, yesterday was an A+ and Wednesday was just a C- and today is a B. Or yesterday was great and today sucked. That's silly to me! Why do we ask people, "How's your day going?" What do we expect them to say? "Well, I have hot water for 364 days a year, but today my water heater broke, so it's the worst day of my life."

I choose to enjoy my life and I choose to live it now. Possibly you've met some people who attempt to live their life in the past. That's one way to live, but it's not how I choose to live. Every day is the best day I've ever had, because it happens now.

When I communicate with someone, I always tell myself, "This is a very important moment." It helps me to focus on the present. Life only happens in the present. Every moment is important. There are no ordinary moments. If you think moments are ordinary, then that's how you created them. Ordinary. Create your moments as very important. Life will slow down for you. You will perform at your best. You'll see life as amazing. Therefore, your life will be amazing.

If you died and had the chance to come back to life for a few moments, how important would those moments be to you? Why do we have to die to understand the concept of creating our moments as very important?

My life has slowed down

Most of the people I talk to say the older they get, the faster life seems to go. However, we also agree that the older we get, the wiser we are. So if we are supposedly wiser, why do we say time goes faster? A minute is still sixty seconds. It always has been sixty seconds. Why does life seem to go by faster and faster? By applying the Reeves Connection Method to my life, I have learned the secret to slowing life down.

Connection has changed my world. My days seem slow and beautiful. I meet so many extraordinary people!

Let me tell a story that illustrates this concept. When I was a teenager I asked a high school baseball coach what I needed to do to be successful in baseball.

He held up a magazine and quickly fanned through the pages. He asked me, "What did you see?"

I said, "I didn't see anything."

He did it a second time and asked me the same thing.

I said, "It's hard to focus on anything, when it goes by that fast.

He said, "That's what baseball is like. You get up to bat and you hear your mom yelling and cheering for you. Your girlfriend is in the stands and you're wondering how your butt looks. The catcher is saying bad things to you and the pitcher looks like he's going to throw the ball at your head. You look at the umpire, and he looks like he doesn't care if you get hit in the head. And here comes the first pitch. You swing at a bad pitch and you miss. The next pitch is right down the middle and you duck out of the way unnecessarily."

The coach said, "You need to be able to see the pitches come at you slowly. You need to be able to count the stiches on the baseball. But you will never be able to see the pitches come at you slowly until you learn to turn all the distractions off."

I said, "Okay. I will work on that."

I was a miserable batter. I could not turn off the distractions and the fears. However, I never forgot this lesson.

While performing interrogations I had to learn to be focused. Imagine performing an interrogation and being distracted. That would not work very well. I have to turn off all the distractions. Sometimes a small gesture or a micro expression is the difference between being able to tell if someone is being truthful or deceptive. I have to be focused.

I have taken that same skill and learned how to apply it to my everyday life. I focus on the conversation I am having with the person in front of me and I focus on the moment that is before me. It is this focus that has allowed my life to seem to slow down. My days are slow and beautiful. I see life come at me slowly. And like the baseball players, I see the pitches of life come at me slowly. I know when to swing and I know when to let the bad pitches go.

When someone asks me a question, I am able to focus on the person and give them my full attention. I see the person as extraordinary and I see the moment as very important. I focus on the person and the moment in the same way a baseball player focuses on the stitches of a baseball. Because of my focus on the present, life slows down for me.

You actually *can* slow your perception of life down. Let me give you an example:

I was in a car accident about a year ago. As soon as the other car hit me on the freeway, I looked in my rear view mirror and glanced on either side of me. I can recall where each and every car was, the color of each car, and how close they were to me. I was also able to keep an eye on the car that hit me as it spun out of control behind me to the left. While all of this was happening I was controlling my car, which was skidding sideways. I was able to bring my car under control out of the skid, even though I was in pain. I was paying attention! At that moment I was not thinking about anything else. I was only thinking about what was happening around me. It was as if the moment slowed down for me and I remember everything.

Other accident victims often say the same thing about their accidents. They say it is as if everything slowed down and they saw the accident in slow motion.

Think about your life and how fast it goes. Remember when I told the baseball coach that it was hard to focus on the pages of the magazine, as he fanned through it so fast? Our life can feel just like that.

It's Monday and you've got a project to finish by Friday at noon. You have 14 messages on your phone. Your spouse is mad at you for missing your child's baseball game last week. So you know you better not miss the game this week. You have 120 emails in your inbox. Someone comes into your office to ask a question and you keep glancing at your computer screen while they are talking to you. You are trying to multi task to accomplish anything. You aren't getting enough sleep and you're worried about your health. And there goes your phone again. It's ringing.

When things seem to go by you so fast, it's hard to focus on anything. At the end of the day, we're not sure what happened because it went by so quickly.

Most of the distractions are in our heads and in our thoughts. Many of the things we worry about aren't even happening right now!

Would you like to have a long and beautiful day? Do you want to see your life in slow motion so you are able to see the stiches on the baseball when it's traveling toward you at 90 miles an hour? Then focus on the present moment. Create this moment as very important.

The Reeves Connection Method has allowed me to enjoy life. I simply have chosen to see each moment in life as precious and important. I am able to focus on what is happening.

I remember buying a new car. It was the car of my dreams. It was very important to me. I can recall the feeling of driving it for the first time. When I arrived at home for the first time with that new car, I drove around the block a few extra times just to enjoy it. I created it as an important moment. I took care of that car. I polished it and cleaned it often. I put leather conditioner on the seats. I didn't let trash pile up on the floor. It was not an ordinary car. It was very important. It was extraordinary. I loved that car.

In the same way, create each moment as very important and you will take care of it. You will love your moments. They won't seem ordinary. They will be extraordinary and very important.

Dale Reeves

Step Three: Search for Virtues and Values

(How to Connect)

This section is powerful. Once you understand this chapter, it will transform your life.

When we listen, what do we listen for?

That may seem like a strange question, because usually when we listen we simply listen. Maybe we're thinking about something else when we listen. Possibly you're like many people and while someone else is speaking you're thinking about what to say next. Or maybe you hear something someone else says, and it spurs other ideas and thoughts in your mind. Maybe you're listening for what's wrong in the other person's conversation.

We all know *those people* who listen for what is wrong. It's not a very pleasant experience to be around them, especially if they're finding out what's wrong with us! Most of the time we try to stop talking to people who are critical of us, or we argue with them.

At school we may listen for what will be on the test. Most of the time we simply listen.

At conferences, I get strange looks from the audience when I say, "Aim your listening."

When I do an interrogation I have to aim my listening. There are many things I am listening for such as qualifiers, modifiers, body language, facial expressions, micro-expressions, and more. As an interrogator, I listen for all of those things. With the Reeves Connection Method, I aim my listening to discover the other person's virtues and values.

When people shoot a gun they are aiming at a target. People don't just shoot their gun in the air, randomly. That wouldn't be any fun or very safe. When we shoot a gun or an arrow we want to see how close we can get to the target. We concentrate and try as hard as we can to hit the target. Then we study the target to see how close we came to the bullseye.

In sports, athletes aim for a target. In basketball, football, even in track and gymnastics, there is a goal, a target or some way to score that athletes are aiming for. Athletes assertively go for the goal. They don't passively aim for their target. And likewise, when listening, we must assert ourselves and go for the goal. We can't just passively listen. We must be resolute in hitting our goal. We must aim our listening so we can discover people's virtues and values.

Aim for the target and study it to see how close you got. I call this principle, "Search for virtues and values." I tell myself, "I am going to aim my listening for this person's virtues and values." Virtues and values are easy to see when we search for them. A target becomes easier to hit when you aim at it. However, you must aim at it. If you don't aim for the target, you'll probably never hit it.

The hard part of searching for virtues and values is controlling your thoughts to make sure you stay on task. It's easy to get distracted by relating, giving opinions, or letting your mind drift.

People don't just come out and tell you their virtues and values. You need to listen for what is *not being said*. You are listening for clues to discover their virtues and values. Most people don't just walk up to you and say, "Hey, do you want to know my virtues and values?" You must listen for what is behind the words they are saying. You must aim to discover their virtues and values. If you aren't looking, you will never find them.

It's an extraordinary experience when you find someone's virtue or value. You feel as though you understand them, and they feel understood. As I said before, people often tell me, "Finally! Someone who understands me!"

Now you have a possibility of understanding *why* they're upset, or *why* they are happy. The *why* matters, it makes a difference in the understanding.

Remember my story about the third grade teacher? I asked the teacher what she liked best about teaching third grade. Once she thought about it for a minute and came up with *why* she liked teaching third grade, it changed her life. I was searching for her virtues and values. The virtue she expressed was love for the children. When I saw her virtue of love for the children I was in awe of her. When I shared the virtue I saw in her, she understood a new passion for teaching third grade. She was inspired. She recognized the ability she possessed. And this recognition enlivened her and inspired her to continue to make this contribution to the world and a difference in many children's lives.

My definitions:

Virtue: Any quality I admire.

Value: Something in the other person that I consider worthwhile.

I thought a lot about the definition of these two words. Virtues and values are about perception. If you're like most people, you go through your day and you don't search for people's virtues and values. So you start to think that you're surrounded by amateurs. Somedays all you see is the stupid stuff people do. You don't see value in people because you're not looking.

People have a lot of value. People are amazing and they are full of virtues and values.

Think about your children. Is there anything you admire or would consider worthwhile in them? Listen to them tonight and listen for their virtues and values. You will be amazed at what you'll find.

How about your spouse? Is there anything you admire or anything you may consider worthwhile? Listen and see what you actually find. You will be delighted with who they really are.

What about your team at work or other people you work with? Listen and see what is there. Is there anything in them that you may consider worthwhile? I am sure they are full of virtues and values that you've probably never recognized before.

Once you learn to listen for virtues and values it transforms your relationships into something amazing. You will see something new in people, that you've never seen before.

People's virtues and values are in every conversation. However, they are hidden behind what people are saying. Virtues and values are on display, but you have to search for them.

Let's discuss how relationships often develop over time. As time goes on we form opinions and judgments about a person. We start to think we know what they are like. Maybe that person is a spouse, sibling, child, employee, parent or boss.

Once we have enough history with a person, we either put up with what we see or we use nagging and complaining to change them into something just a tad bit nicer. We want them to fit into our opinions and judgments of what they ought to be. We keep working on this and usually we get frustrated with the other person's progress. They may not have bought into being changed. You might feel resistance from them. It's a lot of hard work trying to change someone. It's exhausting.

Even if we enjoy the relationship, there may be a great deal of frustration. Judgement and resistance brings negativity to the relationship.

We talked about time in the last chapter. Time happens now. Everything that has happened before this moment is in the past. Consequently, our relationships are built on the past. Our memories may be from yesterday, last year or from this morning, but they are from the past.

To experience the Reeves Connection Method, you need to take the moment and focus on the present instead of the past. Be present to the person you're with, without any expectations. Don't think about any negatives or positives from the past. Instead create this moment as new.

Create people as extraordinary and see the moment as important and precious. Forget about the past. Search for other people's virtues and values and see them as a new person. It's an amazing experience! Clear your mind of anything from the past and see this person that is with you as new again. Tell yourself, "I am going to aim my listening for something I admire and something I see as worthwhile." You never know what you'll find or what you've been missing.

Most likely, when you met your spouse for the first time, you weren't thinking, "I wonder what's wrong with this one." There is a special attraction to what is new. So, see people as new again.

The following is an extremely advanced concept. You actually *can* create people with virtues and values they don't even have. Pick two virtues and values that you wish the other person had. These should be two virtues or values you don't feel the other person has, but are appropriate for the situation.

You can apply this principle in the following way. Let's say you think the other person is hard to get along with. Pick them as 'ease' or 'fun.' Create what you want and you will see it. Even if you can't find evidence that they have a virtue or value, create one for them. Remember, this is all about creation. People will show up to be the person you created them to be.

This principle is not about changing them. It's not nagging or negotiating with them. If your spouse isn't fun to you anymore, simply tell yourself that you are committed to seeing fun.

Do any of us have all the virtues and values we desire to have? Most of us would like to add a few to our list. Simply add one to someone else's list.

I know this may sound strange, but this works! I've seen it work in my business, my personal life and in over hundreds of interrogations.

Like I said earlier, when I do an interrogation there has been a crime committed. Usually something has been stolen. You may think it's obvious that when I sit down with a suspect I am looking for behavior that is bad. Actually, it's quite the opposite. I am looking for virtues and values. I am searching for good behavior.

We do this with our children. When we see something our child does that is good we reinforce good behavior.

I reinforce good behavior during an interrogation. If I don't see a virtue I consider worth reinforcing, I give them one. Usually they grab it and create themselves as having that virtue.

They admit to behavior that is opposed to the virtue I have given them. If I give them the virtue of integrity, they admit that their behavior didn't show integrity.

So what's the science behind this? The science is based on the chemicals our minds dump into our bodies. When I accuse someone of something such as theft, usually the fight or flight response is felt. This releases adrenalin into the body. The person is usually on edge and ready to argue. They will start putting up a wall between us to protect themselves.

On the other hand, if I recognize a person for a virtue and/or value, or if I give them a virtue, endorphins are released into their body. Endorphins cause a person to be relaxed and it deepens their desire for a connection. The body experiences a similar response to laughter. Laughter releases endorphins and the person is much more relaxed than if adrenalin was released into their body.

When endorphins are released into the other person's body, it's more likely that they will be able to express a desire to do what is right. That's why this method works. You create a desire in the other person to grasp onto the virtue you gave them. You inspire them to greatness.

When you complain about someone, you cause adrenaline to be released in their body because they don't like hearing a complaint about themselves. When you give them a virtue you admire, you cause endorphins to be released in their body.

This isn't solely about adrenalin and endorphins. It's about creation. And creation has power.

As I said before, you create this. This method is not about being passive and letting someone ramble on. You create the moment, but you let them do most of the talking. You lead. Quit looking at evidence and create what you want.

Look at the difference between telling someone to do something and inspiring them to do something:

"Tommy, I need you to show some commitment here. You need to be honest with me. What's up with your grades at school?" This statement would cause Tommy's body to experience a release of adrenalin.

However, the following statement would cause Tommy's body to experience a release of endorphins. "Tommy, you're an extraordinary young man. This is a very important moment. I know you have the virtues of integrity and honesty. Let's come together and have a conversation about your grades. Most of all, I want you to be happy and I want a relationship with you. What do I need to understand about school?"

In this conversation I don't ask Tommy directly about his grades. The question I ask is, "What do I need to understand about school?" This will leave our conversation open so Tommy could tell me about the real issues. Maybe he has a friend who's considering suicide and he's worried about it. Notice, I did not ask about his grades, but I said I wanted to talk about his grades. Tommy knows what I want to talk about. I was clear about it, but I left the conversation open so Tommy can tell me what he's really concerned about. I want to know where the real struggle is. I want to understand the *why* behind the behavior.

Let's go through Tommy's thoughts (in parentheses) during these two conversations. What I, as a dad, really want to know is, "What's up with Tommy's grades?"

Conversation number one: "Tommy, I need you to show some commitment here." (*I* need to show some commitment? Dad, you don't know anything about commitment. Where were you during my ball game last week? You said my participation in sports was important to you.)

"You need to be honest with me." (Yeah, right. Just like when you said you'd be at my ball game. You weren't very honest with me, Dad.)

"What's up with your grades at school?" (I'm in trouble and he's going to ground me. I need to come up with a good excuse.)

Conversation number two: "Tommy, you're an extraordinary young man." (Wow, my dad thinks I'm extraordinary? I don't hear that very often.)

"This is a very important moment." (I better pay attention. He *really* thinks I'm extraordinary?)

"I know you have the virtues of integrity and honesty." (Wow, dad finally gets me. Actually, I am a pretty good kid.)

"Let's come together..." (Okay, I like coming together, usually we are at odds with each other.)

"...and have a conversation with you about your grades." (Yeah, he's right. My grades aren't that good.)

"Most of all, I want you to be happy and I want a relationship with you." (Wow! He wants me to be happy and my dad wants a relationship with me? That's awesome! I did not know that.)

"What do I need to understand about school?" (He called me honest and he said I had integrity. My dad wants a relationship with me. He wants me to be happy. Okay, I can't throw this opportunity away. I'll tell him the truth. I know I could do better in school. Wow, maybe my dad really does believe in me!)

Go through these steps: 1. Create the person you're with as extraordinary. 2. Create this moment as very important. 3. Then simply create them with a virtue and value. Pick anything appropriate to the situation. You will be amazed at how it shows up.

If I'm going to inspire a thief to greatness, I need to perceive their reality in the same way that they perceive it.

In the previous example of the son, Tommy, who was struggling in school, I would need to perceive his reality. I would need to get Tommy to talk about the reason why his grades are not going very well. Yet, I want the conversation to be about the virtues I gave him. I gave him integrity and honesty. He will grab those two virtues and make them his. Although I want to have a conversation about his grades, I don't want him to make up any excuses on his own. I want the conversation to be about the virtues I gave him. I am perceiving his reality. However, I am not resonating to him on his level. I'm bringing him to my thoughts.

What do I mean when I say I'm not resonating to him on his level? If Tommy's thoughts are that his grades are good enough, then I could get into a back and forth battle about his grades. Tommy would say his grades are good enough and I would say that his grades are not good enough. That would be a conversation on his level. This back and forth conversation would be likely to go nowhere. I would have to tell Tommy that his grades need to improve or else. Tommy would probably be resentful. And this would be the beginning of a new rift between the two of us.

But how do I inspire him to greatness and bring him to my thoughts? I don't ask about his grades, but I ask him about what is going on at school. I gave him the two virtues of honesty and integrity. I have inspired Tommy to grab the two virtues, while we have a conversation about what's going on at school. He may say that kids are picking on him, or that his teacher can't control the class. We are discussing the "why" he's struggling at school, instead of arguing about his grades being good enough. Once I know why things aren't going well at school, I can bring him to my thoughts, which are, "Your grades aren't acceptable, but I now understand why. Let's work together on a solution."

When I'm conducting an interrogation with someone, I am searching for a virtue and a value. If I don't see one, I have to give them one. When I give them a virtue or value, I make sure it fits the situation.

If I am dealing with a theft, I will give them integrity, trustworthiness, or honesty. I don't give them the virtue of cheerfulness, fun or curiosity. Even though integrity is the opposite of the behavior they've exhibited, it fits the situation of theft.

The same concept works in a personal conversation. In a relationship that is not going well you could give the other person the virtue of commitment, love, or partnership. The virtue of independence or nobility probably wouldn't fit the situation.

Wherever you apply the Reeves Connection Method, whether in your business or personal life, give the other person an appropriate virtue or value for the situation. You want to give the person you're speaking to a virtue that would cause them to say to themselves, "I wish I had more of that virtue in this situation."

Most people have a hard time grasping this concept. Try this exercise. Look around the room and make a mental note about what you see.

After making a mental note about what you see, tell yourself you are searching for the color red. Notice how all of a sudden red shows up. Now tell yourself you do not want to see red. And as you can see, red continues to show up.

Now, tell yourself you are committed to seeing the color blue. Look around the room and amazingly, blue shows up. Now tell yourself you do not want to see any more blue. And when you look around the room, blue is still what you see. It's surprisingly hard to stop seeing something you've been focused on. It's all in your focus.

In just the same way, when you try to change someone's behavior, the very thing you are trying to get rid of shows up again and again. Creating something new is the way to transform your situation. Don't say, "I wish they'd stop nagging me." But do say, "I create the virtue of kindness in them." There is power in what you create.

People have told me that when they tried to stop smoking it was the hardest thing they ever had to do. They finally had success when they created a new activity. They replaced the activity of smoking with something new. Likewise, replace the activity or the behavior you don't like with something new. When you grasp this concept it will transform your life.

I used to tell myself that when it came to driving a car, I was surrounded by amateurs and bad drivers. I thought that everyone should be a safe driver. I'm not saying I had an issue with road rage, but I could get pretty upset when someone pulled out in front of me and I had to slam on my brakes. I have been known to yell in the car, "What! Are you trying to kill us?"

Driving was not a relaxing or fun task. It wasn't that I hated driving, it was just that I noticed every bad habit of other drivers, such as not using their blinkers. I finally saw that I was being a victim of my thoughts about driving. First of all, I realized I had unrealistic expectations. Thinking that everyone should be a safe driver is not realistic. Now I tell myself, "Look at all the cars on the road. Thousands of cars and drivers are on the freeway. Most days I get to work without a scratch. That's incredible! Look at all these safe drivers."

I don't have the unrealistic expectations that everyone should be a safe driver anymore. I understand that I need to drive defensively and that other drivers will sometimes make mistakes.

If someone pulls out in front of me and I have to slam on the brakes, I don't get all bent out of shape over it. It doesn't change my mood. I actually enjoy the moments when I'm in traffic. Now I create people as extraordinary drivers. And that's exactly what I see, extraordinary drivers.

I simply chose to create something different. I created myself surrounded by amazing and safe drivers. Now I have a completely different experience when driving a car.

Most of us would deny being prejudiced. However, if you look honestly at your everyday interactions, most of us have not gotten rid of constant everyday judgments. Many of us have labels for people that are different from us. Labels such as "irritating," "high maintenance," "closed minded," and "perfectionist." Most of us aren't psychologists and yet I hear people label others as OCD, or ADHD. We may think we *know it all* about other people. Nevertheless, we only see what we think we know. Maybe there's something we're not seeing.

For example some of us might call perfectionism a disease or a syndrome. However, we depend on our pharmacist or our neurosurgeon to be a perfectionist. All I'm trying to say is, let's ignore any past judgments we may have about a person and focus on the present. Create what you want to focus on and you will see it.

I was at the doctor's office and I was speaking to a health care professional. She told me she was OCD. She said, "I have to do the dishes every night before going to bed."

I asked, "Have you been diagnosed with OCD?"

She replied, "No, but I can tell I have it because I *can't* go to bed without doing the dishes first."

I said, "It sounds like waking up to a clean kitchen would be a wonderful place to live. I'm not sure that's a disease. However, waking up to a dirty kitchen every morning could be a foodborne illness problem."

She said, "I never thought of that."

Just because a person likes to do the dishes every night before going to bed doesn't mean they are OCD. Possibly they just like things to be in order. Maybe they love cleanliness. Maybe they love routines. We would like the neighborhood restaurant to love cleanliness, wouldn't we?

When we want to get away with something, a few of us create the other person with a disease or syndrome. For example, if someone keeps nagging us to pick up our socks off the floor. We might say, "Oh, you're just OCD!" Sometimes labeling people gives us an excuse to act the way we want.

Here's how the Mayo Clinic defines OCD: *Obsessive-compulsive disorder (OCD) features a pattern of unreasonable thoughts and fears (obsessions) that lead you to do repetitive behaviors (compulsions). These obsessions and compulsions interfere with daily activities and cause significant distress.* *www.mayoclinic.org*

Asking someone to pick up their socks probably isn't OCD. But I'm not a psychologist.

I was talking to an assistant manager at a retail store. He told me that his boss said he would always be an assistant manager because he was too ADHD to ever manage a store. I told the assistant manager, "To me, it looks like you successfully manage many things at the same time."

He said, "Really? Do you think I could manage a store someday?" He continued, "I do work hard. But my boss says I'll never make it."

I said, "Absolutely! You'll make it. You work hard. You are kind to people and you're a great leader with your crew. You keep an eye on the whole store, while at the same time getting your tasks done. You have the virtues of teamwork and commitment."

Immediately, the assistant manager stood up straighter and looked more confident. Over the next weeks and months he showed increasing confidence in himself. Having someone believe in him seemed to make a big difference.

One year later he did become a store director. And he's an awesome store director! All I did was have a short conversation with him and recognize him for his virtues and values.

Maybe someone in your life is grouchy every day. Remember, we find what we are looking for. Let's try creating something out of nothing. Try this. Be assertive and tell yourself, "I create this person as kind." And just like the color red in our earlier exercise, kindness will show up overwhelmingly. Or you can choose to be a victim and look for evidence to prove this person *is* grouchy. Either way, you are creating it.

I apply the principle of searching for virtues and values when I interview and interrogate people. I sit before thieves and I create them as extraordinary people. I don't see them as thieves. I see them as being the way I create them to be, extraordinary. I talk to criminals, and it would be easy to see them as bad people. But instead, I create them with virtues and values. I search for their virtues and values first. When I don't find one, I give them one.

Creating people takes work. It takes focus. It goes against our everyday survival instinct. We have an instinct to complain and to feel like victims. Creating is hard work at first, but soon it will become second nature.

Let me give an example with a story.

I had to Interview and interrogate a man who worked in a retail store. He had a second job as a fireman. After a few minutes of conversation I chose a virtue for him. I said, "You're an extraordinary man and this is a very important moment. You have the virtue of integrity. You're a fireman. You are the last profession that everyone loves. Sadly, some people don't trust doctors, and some don't trust cops, and yet others don't trust clergy. But a fireman is the last profession that everyone trusts and loves. You have integrity."

He said to me, "There are some things I've done wrong."

I said, "I don't want to talk about right and wrong. I want to talk about you restoring your integrity. When you walk out of here today I believe you will be able to take a deep breath and know that you have restored your integrity."

This man confessed to eleven thousand dollars of theft, a lot more than we knew about. (We had not yet had a chance to review all of the evidence.) Because I created him with integrity, he showed up with integrity.

Three days later he called me and said, "This may sound strange, but thank you for catching me. I am a better man today because of you. You saw something inside of me that I had forgotten about. You saw me better than I saw myself. Thank you."

He then said, "I'll have the restitution for the company in a few weeks."

He called me three weeks later and we met at a coffee shop. He handed me a check for eleven thousand dollars. He repaid his debt to the store in full.

He said, "Thank you again for seeing the real person I was. I am a better person today because of you. I had lost who I really was, but you brought me back." He told me about his new job and how he had already advanced at the fire station in just a few short weeks since we last spoke. I saw a new light in this man's eyes.

Back when I first sat down to interview the firefighter, I didn't see integrity in him. He acted cocky and had a negative attitude. I gave him the virtue of integrity. He stole from us. He was a thief. But I created him as having integrity, solely based on his job as a firefighter. And he became integrity. He restored his integrity, and therefore restored the person he desired to be. I created that. You also have the ability to create virtues and values in the people you meet every day.

We don't have to look at evidence or look at our opinions to make a decision or a judgement about someone's character. Just create the other person with a virtue or value and it will show up. Some of us are already creating the other person with a complaint or a disease. Just switch it to a virtue or value.

The inspiration the fireman experienced lasted much longer than just a few hours. Why does the Reeves Connection Method have a lasting effect on people? The answer is fairly simple. Most of us have heard inspiring stories about other people. By hearing an inspirational story about someone else, we feel the emotion of being inspired. For most of us that feeling only lasts a short time, sometimes only a few hours.

But when you use the Reeves Connection Method and recognize a virtue in someone, or give that person a new virtue, the inspirational story is about themselves. It is personal. They are the subject of the inspirational story. It's about them. You personalized the story to their real lives. They see themselves anew, with the virtue you gave to them.

The inspiration is lasting because they recognize new potential, confidence and ability in themselves. They realize that they can make a difference in the world. Possibly they realize this for the first time in their lives. Therefore the inspiration is life-changing.

You inspired them to greatness. Remember my definition of greatness: When someone recognizes the potential, confidence and ability they possess. And this recognition enlivens them and inspires them to make a contribution to the world and a difference in people's lives.

What about you?

Now, create a virtue and value in yourself, based on nothing. In other words, we usually tell ourselves that we are strong in certain areas. Therefore we create something out of a strength we already believe we have. But this time, pick something new. Ask yourself, who do I *want* to be?

Do you want to be integrity? Then create yourself as integrity. Tell yourself that you are integrity. And you will make decisions that prove you do have integrity.

Tell yourself that you are commitment and you will make decisions surrounded by a new commitment toward your goals. Don't wait until you have evidence that you are a committed person. Do it now.

I created myself as connection. Therefore I connect with people. My strength has always been hard work and getting results. And although the seeds of connection were part of my tool set, connection wasn't my strength. I wasn't good at it until I created myself as connection. Now

I connect with people because that is who I am. I look at someone and tell myself that they are extraordinary and this is an important moment. Therefore, I am going to aim my listening to discover their virtues and values.

I made a choice to use my new virtue of connection in my job and business. I didn't perfect the method until becoming a CFI. The Reeves Connection Method changed my life. I became exceptional at my job of interview and interrogation.

Before I took my current position, the previous three people who'd held my position seemed to struggle with this job. They didn't last very long in the job. That's because of the difficulty of being effective as an interrogator in stopping theft, while also being able to maintain positive relationships throughout a large company.

When I accepted my current position, I knew I had to create something new.

The Reeves Connection Method has enabled me to have positive relationships throughout the company while also being effective at addressing crime. This method has also changed my life.

If you keep telling a child that they are bad, they usually exhibit bad behavior. If you keep telling yourself that you are bad, you will probably become exactly as you created yourself. Give yourself a virtue that is worthy of an extraordinary life. Create yourself and others as something amazing! Remember, you will always be who you create yourself to be.

See the best in other people and see the best in yourself. Forget the bad things you may have seen in others and forgive freely. Forget the bad things you've done. Take a deep breath and focus on other people's virtues and values.

Create your world, not out of the past, but out of the present moment.

Everything you've seen, everywhere you've been and everything you've experienced is in the past. It happened before now. See today as new. Every moment is new again and again. So what should you do with this new moment? Search for other people's virtues and values. It will transform your world into something beautiful.

You are already creating things. My challenge to you is to create things that you want to live with. Create people as people you desire to be around.

With the Reeves Connection Method we will stop looking for evidence. It's always easy to find evidence to support our viewpoints, but this world is complex and things aren't always what they seem. It's likely that, given enough time and new information, both our opinions and the opinions of those we disagree with will change. I know my opinions have changed in many ways since I was a teen.

It is usually easier to come up with a few of our own faults than a few virtues. And likewise, it's usually easier to pick out someone else's faults than to see what virtues and values they have. That is why you have to focus on searching for virtues and values. Be assertive and search. Search for virtues and values during a conversation and you will create a connection.

Search for virtues and values, instead of trying to relate or giving opinions.

This book is not about how to connect with people we already have a lot in common with. This book is about how to connect with anybody. We can make meaningful connections with people whose viewpoints are opposite to ours. We must look for the values that lie behind people's behavior. Behind someone's passion for a different viewpoint there are many values to find. When I connect with someone, I don't bring up our differences. I look for things I admire.

Our minds run on auto pilot and they are trying to automatically relate to people. Usually we don't automatically listen for virtues and values. Our minds search for what is wrong and formulate opinions quickly, even when we don't have much evidence.

Create people as powerful and create a world you want to live in. We will all be better off because of you. You will start to make a difference in the world. We will all be happier because of your creation.

I sit before thieves and I see them as having integrity. They confess to me and they thank me for seeing the beauty that is within their souls. Because I create them with integrity, they become integrity.

If I can see a thief as extraordinary, surely you can see ordinary people as extraordinary. Let's go change the world together.

See the value in a connection.

Here is an example of an everyday conversation I had just today:

I'll begin with a little background. A few months ago I connected with a loan officer who helped me get a loan on my house. During that conversation I noticed a painting behind her desk and I asked her about it. She told me she painted it.

"Wow," I said, "You are really talented!"

She said, "I went to college to major in art."

I asked her, "What are you currently painting?"

She said, "I lost all my creativity. I'm not inspired to paint anything anymore."

I said, "What would it take for you to be inspired to paint again?"

She said, "I don't know, I think my painting days are over."

I said, "You are highly talented. I'd love to see your next project when it is finished."

She just smiled at me and helped me with my loan.

This afternoon I was walking by her office and she came out to say hi to me. I smiled at her.

She excitedly told me, "I started my next painting and I'm really excited about it."

I replied, "That's wonderful. I can't wait to see it. What is it about?"

She said, "It has to do with the rebirth of old goals."

I said, "I'm so proud of you. You are a business person and an artist. Not only do you have the virtues of professionalism, kindness and knowledge about business, but you also have the virtue of creativity. That's an incredible combination. And you're painting again! You have made my day!"

Her eyes began to tear up and she could hardly talk. She muttered a sincere "Thank you! That means a lot to me." I am sure she will remember this conversation for a long time.

During our conversation I was listening for her virtues and values. I was not looking for a chance to relate. It was truly a joy to touch her life for a moment in a meaningful way and to see how our previous conversation moved and inspired her to take action.

Conversations like this flow naturally for me and I look forward to seeing the amazing virtues and values in others. The Reeves Connection Method brings more color and joy into my life and makes my days full and meaningful.

This conversation had an impact on my life as well. It was an extraordinary experience to watch this businesswoman and artist come alive with expression. When we recognize someone for their virtues and values, this creates an amazing moment of connection. People feel as though someone in this world "gets them." Who they are in this world is understood for a moment. When someone recognizes something inside of us, a little spark goes off. This spark is energizing for both people in the conversation.

Discover people as new again.

In a sense, when you connect with somebody you are actually discovering them. You may see them deeper and recognize more in them than they would have ever seen in themselves. When you look for people's virtues and values, you will find virtues and values. When you acknowledge a human being for their virtues and values, many times, you show them something new about themselves.

They may have felt as though they were a loving person, but hearing it from someone else, energizes a spark of connection that ignites greatness. You not only energize a relationship through this, but you inspire the other person to greatness! When people are inspired to greatness they start believing in themselves. In this moment lives are changed.

Search for virtues and values in your team at work.

When people are inspired to greatness they have a strong desire to do the right things.

If you own a business or are a manger, and you connect to your team with the Reeves Connection Method, your team will feel like an owner in your business. People don't normally steal from themselves.

When you acknowledge a team member for a virtue or value, you inspire them to greatness. When you inspire greatness in team members, you empower them. Empowered team members create extraordinary things. An empowered team is highly productive.

If employees in a business could connect with each other, how far could sales and profits go? If the back-biting and complaining stopped, what could be possible? An empowered team could transform your business into something extraordinary.

Talk about the virtues and values you see in people.

After having a conversation with someone, most of us would never say to ourselves, "Wow, I showed love and understanding to that person today. I'd like to recognize myself for my passion and my desire to help this person. I am sure I was a blessing to them." It would never occur to most of us to say this to ourselves.

When we do something nice for someone else, usually we're just trying to do what's right and help someone out. We rarely see our own virtues and values in action, or at least we don't recognize them in action.

However, it may have a bigger impact on our life if someone else said to us, "Wow, you showed love and understanding to me today. I would like to acknowledge you for your passion and desire to help my cause. You have truly been a blessing to me." This would have a greater impact on our lives than if we said it to ourselves.

Most of us are usually too hard on ourselves. When someone else recognizes our virtues and values, it is very moving. Hearing this from someone else creates an extraordinary moment. A moment of connection inspires people to greatness.

Focus on virtues and values. Be assertive

I am assertive when I tell a suspect, "I see you have integrity." They never say, "What are you talking about, I don't have any integrity." Usually they sit up straighter and they start to believe they have a chance at having integrity instead of only wishing they had it. They start to listen to me intently because I see something in them that they wish they had more of. They begin to see that I believe in them.

This brings a connection to the conversation and helps us resolve a conflict.

This simple method causes people to be honest with me and therefore they confess to the crime they have committed. Not only do they confess, but they offer their confession willingly. I hear quite often, "I was stupid and I took money that wasn't mine."

Even if I say, "Are you sure it was you?" They say, "Yes. I want to take the first step in getting my life back on track. It was me."

It is amazing to see the results of this method of connection. When I recognize the value of integrity in a suspect, they convict themselves and offer a confession.

You have to give your mind something to focus on. Tell your mind the person before you is an extraordinary person. Tell your mind to pause and look around. Be present, because this is a very important moment. Then tell your mind to search for virtues and values. Be assertive with your mind and take control of it. You will be amazed at what you will find.

Virtue Exercise

Let me repeat my definitions for the purpose of this exercise.

My definitions:

Virtue: Any quality I admire.

Value: Something in the other person that I consider worthwhile.

When you are searching for virtues, you are aiming for any quality you admire. When you are searching for values, you are aiming for something in the other person that you consider worthwhile. You should be able to find a virtue in *my list of virtues*, that will help you discover something you admire or consider worthwhile in others.

In the advanced concept of giving someone a virtue or value, make sure you pick something that fits the situation.

During my seminar on connection, I sometimes ask people in the class to come up with as many virtues and values as they can. Most people can only give me about 10 to 12 virtues and values for life. I came up with the following list, so we can all see that there are many virtues and values in life.

Dale Reeves

I have come to realize that the reason some people don't think about searching for people's virtues is because they think there are only about 10 of them. And the person they are speaking to might not have any of those 10. Maybe most of us don't realize that there are numerous virtues to choose from. I have listed over 100 virtues. There are many more virtues than those I have listed. Please add more to this list. Add some virtues that are important to you.

I would like you to read my list of virtues. I put my definitions of each virtue after the name of the virtue. My challenge to you, is for you to add your own definition to each virtue. Add and take away whatever you want.

Like I said before, virtues are about perception. For example, if the person you are helping doesn't think you are acting in a helpful way, this person won't think you have the virtue of helpfulness. Perception matters.

As an interrogator, I have to be aware of how I am being perceived by the suspect. It doesn't matter if I am being genuine or not, if the suspect doesn't think I am genuine. Consider that the way people perceive us, is their experience of reality. When looking to connect with someone, it doesn't matter how we perceive ourselves in the conversation. What matters is how the other person perceives us. If you want to inspire someone, you have to be very mindful of how they are perceiving you and your actions.

Think of a person that is in your life right now. Then read the list and write down the virtues you feel this person has. Then ask yourself this question, "Have you ever thanked them for these virtues?

Let's say you have a person that you work with that keeps their head down and works hard, but they don't really do anything you would consider amazing. They show up on time and do the job that is expected. They work well with others. We could easily see that they have the virtues of workability, teamwork, cooperation and dependability. You might also easily see that they are not assertive, brave or decisive.

Sometimes we are tempted to judge someone on the basis of the virtues we have. Just because someone doesn't have the virtues we possess, doesn't mean they don't have any virtues.

Which list do we focus on? The list of virtues they possess, or the list of virtues they don't have?

To connect and make a difference in someone's life, you must focus on the list of virtues they possess. If you focus on the list of virtues that they don't have, then you are focused on what is wrong with this person. You are judging them, and you won't produce the positive results of inspiring them to greatness.

Most of the time, we just aren't searching for virtues. That's the simple reason we don't find any.

Think of one of your children, your spouse, or a parent. Now read the list of virtues. I'm sure you will find something new to admire about them.

List of Virtues

Acceptance: Finding worth in something, just the way it is.

Accountability: Taking full responsibility. Not afraid to be audited or questioned.

Appreciation: Expressing gratitude.

Assertiveness: Taking charge. Not afraid to make things happen.

Awe: Having wonder and respect for a creation.

Bravery: Acting with character in the midst of fear.

Caring: Having heart and feeling for those in need, then taking action.

Cautious: Showing patience and safety. Taking care and showing vigilance.

Charity: Giving without expectations.

Cheerfulness: Noticeably happy. Optimistic.

Cleanliness: An environment of order. Unsoiled.

Closeness: A desire to have a close relationship with someone. To be in sync with someone. Connected and having intimacy with someone.

Commitment: Promise, obligation and duty that shows up in your calendar as action. More than just a wish or a desire.

Community: Being part of, and having the desire to contribute to, a larger group.

Compassion: Having empathy for others. Showing kindness.

Confidence: Assurance in oneself in taking action.

Connection: Showing care for relationships. Respect for, and association with other people. Absence of division.

<u>Considerate</u>: Showing care and kindness to another person through action.

<u>Consideration</u>: Looking at two or more sides before making a decision. Being thoughtful.

<u>Contentment</u>: Being happy with what you have. Gratification grounded in peacefulness.

<u>Cooperation</u>: Teamwork, where others ideas and goals are completed, without judgement or opinion.

<u>Courage</u>: Action in the midst of fear.

<u>Courtesy</u>: Speaking and acting in a kind and gracious way. Showing the importance and significance of others through action.

<u>Create</u>: Powerful transformation constructed in the midst of nothing.

<u>Curiosity</u>: A strong desire to learn something.

<u>Decisiveness</u>: Making firm decisions based on the data currently available.

<u>Defiance</u>: Resistance in action, against the status quo.

<u>Dependability</u>: Reliable, trustworthy, and loyal. Can be counted on to get the job done.

Determination: Firmness of purpose that cannot be thwarted.

Devotion: Committed to action and loyalty. Zeal for another person or principle.

Dignity: Honoring people's virtues and values no matter what.

Diligence: Action done consistently and at the best of your ability.

Discernment: Taking care to investigate appropriately and without favoritism.

Discrete: Without gossip. Without communication of judgement.

Efficient: Taking action, in a way that uses resources wisely, while quickly attaining a goal.

Endurance: Consistently able to have stamina. Acting as though obstacles are only part of the process.

Enthusiasm: Eagerness, fervor and passion toward something.

Excellence: 100% of our best. A state of mind.

Experience: Skill in completing a task with excellence because of practice and diligence.

Extraordinary: Astonishing excellence.

Fairness: Making sure each side is heard. Impartiality.

Faith: Hope and assurance in things not yet seen.

Family: A team that acts with love, accountability and understanding toward each other. A team that connects and works together.

Faithfulness: Unwavering belief in something cherished. Believing and taking action despite circumstances.

Fidelity: Faithfulness in our relationships in the midst of any circumstance.

Focus: Consistent attention. Concentration on the goal.

Forbearance: Showing acts of faithfulness and loyalty, in the midst of troubling circumstances.

Forgiveness: A commitment which gives up the chance to ever bring up or judge any wrongdoing again.

Fortitude: The will to act toward your goal and withstand troubles, no matter what. Strength of character.

Friendliness: Acts of kindness and reaching out to others with warmth.

Fun: Ability to experience joy and laughter. Enjoyable experience.

Generosity: Giving freely without prejudice, even when you don't have enough for yourself.

Gentleness: Moving moderately and wisely.

Grace: Giving respect and admiration to someone who is undeserving.

Gratitude: The act of freely expressing appreciation.

Greatness: When someone recognizes the potential, confidence and ability they possess. And this recognition inspires them to make a contribution to the world and a difference in people's lives.

Helpfulness: Work with action, which makes a difference to others.

Honesty: Non-deceptive. Truthful. Sincere.

Honor: Highly respect. Esteem.

Hope: Belief and desire for something expected.

Humble: Modest. Without complaint.

Idealism: Aiming for a standard of perfection. Envisioning something better.

Impartiality: Objective. Without judgement.

Independence: Self-reliance. Separate from undue influence. Making our own choices.

Initiative: Resourcefulness. Taking action on our own.

Inspirational: Exhibiting a quality that causes enthusiasm in others.

Integrity: Whole. Reliable. Honest. Able to hold the load without complaint. Doing what we say we will do.

Joyfulness: Inner sense of peace and happiness.

Justice: Impartiality. Consistent fairness. Appropriate response.

Kindness: Tender attention. Friendly, helpful and well-meaning.

Love: Care, acceptance and affinity for someone just as they are. Highly valuing something or someone.

Loyalty: Unwavering faithfulness and commitment. Steadfast in allegiance. Faithful to a person, or duty.

Majestic: Great and impressive dignity.

Mercy: Freely blessing someone instead of punishing them for their offense.

Mindfulness: Thoughtful awareness of the impact of our action upon others and the world.

Moderation: Self-discipline to create balance in our lives. The avoidance of extremes in actions, judgments, advice or opinions. Conquering our misplaced passions.

Modesty: Self-respect and quiet confidence.

Nobility: Having high moral standards. Doing the right thing without any thought of complaint.

Obedience: Following orders and the law. Compliance to authority.

Openness: Willingness to communicate and consider new ideas. Listening to others with humility and sincerity, despite disagreement.

Orderliness: Taking action methodically. Creating an environment of organization.

Partnership: To work together toward common goals. Having a stake in a common outcome.

Passion: Strong emotion and enthusiasm.

Patience: Waiting peacefully. Ability to endure delay. Tolerating suffering without getting upset.

Peacefulness: Resolving conflict in a just and gentle way. Freedom from mental agitation. Undisturbed.

Perceptive: Clarity of insight. Aware and sensitive.

Perseverance: Never giving up on goals and dreams. Staying the course, no matter what.

Prudence: Wise in conduct. Shrewd or thrifty in future plans.

Purity: Ability to abide by our own compass. Free from outside influences. Free from contamination.

Purposefulness: Clear vision of the goal with steadfast action.

Reliability: Dependable. Consistently good in quality. Trustworthy.

Respect: Honoring others through our words and actions. Treating others with courtesy and dignity.

Responsibility: Accountable and true to ourselves and others. Action that makes a positive difference in other's lives.

Reverence: Deep respect. Living with wonder and faith. Reflection of, and devotion to, absolute truth.

Righteousness: Impeccable integrity to absolute truth.

Sacrifice: Giving up what is important to us for the betterment of others.

Safety: Being careful and diligent not to have an accident.

Sensitivity: Being aware of how our actions and judgements affect others. Heightened awareness.

Serenity: Tranquility of spirit. Peacefulness that shows strength.

Service: Contribution toward others in the giving of our time and duty.

Sincerity: Genuine. Free from deceitful actions.

Spontaneity: Unplanned action.

Steadfastness: Persevering, with the strength to remain true to our purpose, in spite of obstacles that arise.

Strength: Inner power and endurance. Ability to focus on the blessings in our lives in the midst of worry or trouble.

Tact: Kindness toward others when speaking about opinions and judgments. Sensitivity with thoughtfulness.

Temperance: Discerning what to say, when to say it and what is better left unsaid. Moderate restraint. Being thoughtful in our speech and our actions.

Tenacity: Never giving up.

Thankfulness: Showing gratitude.

Tolerance: Being open to differences in opinions. Refraining from judgments. Accepting others thoughts about a concept with grace.

Toughness: Strong, durable and not easily destroyed.

Tranquility: Peaceful. Undisturbed.

Trust: Conviction of faith without doubt. Lacking suspicion.

Trustworthiness: Being worthy. Reliable.

Truthfulness: Honest and without deception.

Understanding: Giving others the chance to express themselves and the chance to explain until mutual thoughts of the same concept occur. Listening with compassion acceptance and accuracy to others. Seeing the virtues and values behind the words that are spoken.

Unity: Inclusiveness. Finding common ground in our diversity.

<u>Uprightness</u>: Living in integrity. Doing justice for the sake of justice, not for personal gain.

<u>Wisdom</u>: The gift of making wise decisions. Using intelligence, knowledge and understanding with common sense.

<u>Workability</u>: Practical ability to make a contribution toward a job or task. Honest and trustworthy.

<u>Zeal</u>: Passionate enthusiasm for a cause or for life.

Remember to think of a specific person and then read this list of virtues. I am sure you will find something new in the other person that you can admire.

Create something new by searching for virtues and values.

On page 195 is a virtue search worksheet. Instructions follow...

Instructions:

One: Write down the name of someone that comes to mind.

Two: List the virtues the person already has.

Three: List a few virtues the person does not have.

Four: Create this person as having one or two new virtues. Make sure the new virtues fit the situation and relationship you are in with this person.

You will see new beauty in the person you have selected. You should see new virtues in this person, virtues you didn't see before.

Don't focus on the virtues they don't have. It can be helpful to write down virtues that are not part of their personality. Then we can realize that we can't expect everyone to have every virtue. Sometimes someone with assertiveness doesn't have patience. And someone with patience doesn't have assertiveness. That's fairly simple to understand.

When you create a new virtue in the other person, make sure you acknowledge them for the new virtue. Say something like, "Sam, I clearly see that you have the virtue of service and family. I appreciate your contribution toward us in this family."

Virtue Search Worksheet

Name_____

Virtues this Person Already Has

_____   _____   _____

_____   _____   _____

_____   _____   _____

_____   _____   _____

_____   _____   _____

_____   _____   _____

Virtues This Person Does Not Have

_____   _____   _____

_____   _____   _____

I Create This Person Having the Virtues of:

(Make sure these virtues fit the situation)

_____   _____

Dale Reeves

Step Four: Listen and Lead

(How to Connect)

Conversations often go like this. Two people meet and exchange greetings. One person talks for a while. This person talks about what they've been up to. Then the second person relates to a subject the first person has brought up. The second person tells the first some anecdotes and stories related to the topic the first person was speaking about. This may stimulate some further ideas in the first person to share another story from their past.

Both people are telling each other about experiences and ideas that put themselves in a favorable light. In other words, they are talking about things that make themselves look good. Often the two people settle on a conclusion they can both agree about. "This process is crazy" or "Yeah, kids are like that" or "Won't this weather ever change?"

Both people relate, give opinions and make judgments. It's just a normal conversation.

The conversation is usually about things that neither person really cares about very deeply. It's a conversation only on the surface. It's not a deep connecting conversation, although it may seem like a connection. At best, it's a surface connection. Maybe both people connected on the topic of the weather. Wow.

What both people don't realize is that they are giving up information about themselves. They are telling someone else what they like and don't like, and it might not even be genuine. They're just talking. Both people are trying to look good (or at least acceptable) to the other person.

The Reeves Connection Method looks at conversations differently. The focus is on making the other person look good, not on making ourselves look good. By focusing on making the other person look good, you can actually go deeper into a more genuine connection, which makes a difference for both people. This connection method is gratifying for both people in the conversation.

In an interrogation, I need to find out information about another person. I don't need to talk about myself. I ask the questions and I allow the other person to give me information. I want them to feel good about themselves. I want them to feel comfortable. I want to know how they think and what they think about certain topics. I use this method to make a connection with people while I'm interviewing or interrogating them.

It was life-changing for me when I began to use this method in normal conversations. I learned that I could quickly touch and inspire people, simply by asking questions that allowed the other person to tell me about themselves. I realized that if I didn't relate, or respond with something about myself, the other person would tell me more about themselves.

It is much easier to find virtues and values in another person if I let them talk. When I responded and related, I discovered that finding virtues and values was harder, because the conversation never got very deep. I didn't find many virtues in the topic of the weather.

Listening and leading is a different way of having a conversation. I listen and I ask questions so the other person can look good. I ask questions such as:

Where did you go on vacation last year?

What was your favorite part of the vacation?

If you went back what would you do differently?

What do you do for a job?

What do you like best about your job?

What do you do for fun?

Who painted that painting? (Wow, you're really talented.)

What's your next project?

Where do you live?

What do you like best about where you live?

I ask them questions so they can shine. I don't relate, give my opinion, or make any judgments. I liken this conversation style to ballroom dancing. In ballroom dancing it's the gentleman's job to lead. He decides where the dance is going and it's the lady's job to look good. He provides the frame and she looks good in the picture.

In conversations, I ask the questions and the other person responds. I ask questions that make them look good. Listening and leading is an amazing experience and it's not that hard. You would naturally listen and lead if you were sitting next to your favorite celebrity.

Remember. We create the other person as extraordinary. We create this moment as a very important moment. We aim our listening toward searching for virtues and values.

And now we listen and lead. Since this is an extraordinary person, we naturally want to know about them.

Let me explain with a story. One Sunday evening I decided to take my wife out for coffee. It had been a busy week and we hadn't had a chance to be together.

We walked into the coffee shop and ordered two drinks. I have a bad habit of looking around the room when I'm in a public place. This must be from my days as a police officer. Usually I take a chair against the back wall so I can see everyone in the cafe. But I really wanted to focus on my wife and give her my attention so I picked a table at the back. I sat with my back toward the front door so all I could see was my wife and the wall.

After about an hour of great discussion and connection with each other, my wife excused herself to go to the restroom. Earlier, I had seen an older gentleman walk past the window and enter the store. He ordered a drink and sat to the left of me on a chair. (I know, I have great peripheral vision.)

After my wife left for the restroom I looked at the man and said, "How's the crossword puzzle going?" He didn't even look up as he said, "If you've done one you've done them all."

That didn't go anywhere, but I was determined to connect with him so I told myself, "This is an extraordinary man. This is a very important moment. I'm going to aim my listening for his virtues and values."

I looked at the man's shoes. His shoes looked old, but they also looked very well cared for. So I said, "Those look like great shoes. It seems as though you've taken good care of them."

He looked up at me and said, "Those are good shoes and they are very comfortable." This was my cue, I am now going to listen and lead. When I listen and lead, I make the other person look good.

I asked, "What do you do?"

He said, "I'm retired."

I asked, "What did you used to do?"

He replied, "I worked with computers."

I asked, "When did you work with computers?"

He replied, "In the seventies."

I said, "Wow that was cutting edge technology in the seventies! What did you do with computers in the seventies?"

He said, "I installed computers in the Iowa State Capitol in Des Moines, Iowa."

I leaned a little closer to him and asked, "How long did that take you to install computers back in the seventies?"

He replied, "It took me three years to install the computers and to train the people."

I asked, "So, did you live in Des Moines or stay in a hotel?"

He said, "I moved there. I lived there for three years."

I asked, "What street did you live on?" He told me what street he lived on. I know the exact street! I lived in Des Moines for four years. I was tempted to relate to him, but I knew we'd end up talking about neighborhoods in Des Moines, and that would have only been a surface connection at best. So, I focused on my desire to connect with the man. I pushed back my inclination to relate, and I asked, "What was it like training people?"

He said, "Well, we didn't have Windows 95 and we didn't have the drag and drop stuff." He paused and looked at my face and asked, "Do I know you?"

I said, "No. I've never met you before."

And he said, "You remind me of a good friend of mine."

I asked, "What is your friend like?"

The old man looked ten years younger as he straightened up in his chair and said, "He's dead now. But he used to have a machine shop. He could make all kinds of things! He was contacted by NASA. NASA was having trouble with the Lunar Module. NASA asked him if he could machine a part for them. My friend made a part for the Lunar Module. The part he made helped the Lunar Module land on the moon. That part he made is still on the moon today!"

I said, "It sounds like you admire him." He went on for a few minutes talking about his old friend and the interesting times they'd spent in his friend's shop. His face lit up and he got excited while telling me his stories. I enjoyed seeing the excitement in this extraordinary man's face. I felt like I had a glimpse into the early space age and the early computer age. I enjoyed sharing in the old man's memories.

Then he looked at me again and asked, "Are you sure I don't know you?"

I said, "Yes. I'm pretty sure we've never met before, but it sure is great talking to you."

My wife came out of the restroom and the three of us connected for a few more minutes. When I stood up to leave I said, "You are an extraordinary man! Thank you for sharing your life with me for a moment. I enjoyed your computer stories and hearing about your friend. Thank you for your contributions to our society."

His face lit up as he smiled and said, "Thank you."

As my wife and I walked out of the coffee shop she put both of her hands on my arm and said, "He got to spend a few minutes with his old friend, didn't he?"

"Yes," I said, "I supposed he did."

I really enjoyed my conversation with this gentleman. Think about it. If you go to a coffee shop on a Sunday evening to do a crossword puzzle, it's likely that you're lonely and just want to be around some people.

All I did was create this man as extraordinary. I created the moment as important. I searched for virtues and values. And then, I listened and led the conversation.

I found a value in him, just by looking at his shoes and how well he took care of them. I saw the value of caring for quality. Even though the man was old, and walked with a cane, I saw the virtue of strength. He sure loved and valued his friend who could make high-quality items. He had a zeal for life.

If we search for virtues and values, we will find them. We usually find what we listen for. If we listen for what is wrong, we will find something wrong. If we listen for something to relate to, we will find that. Once you decide on a virtue or value, that fits the other person and the situation, just listen and lead. This older gentleman was extraordinary.

Notice, I was assertive. I led the conversation. Listening and leading is not about being passive. I asked the questions that allowed this older gentleman to look good. As in a ballroom dance, I chose the moves so my partner could look good. I was in charge. I was the lead.

I listened and I led the conversation so the man could tell me about himself. I also acknowledged him. Acknowledgment is step five.

My wife asked me later, "Why did you connect with him? Was it because he looked lonely?"

I responded, "Absolutely not! I didn't see him as anything apart from extraordinary. I didn't see him as lonely or as needing anything. He may have come into the coffee shop because he didn't want to be alone at home, but that isn't why I spoke to him. I simply saw him as extraordinary and created this moment as very important."

She said, "But you can't do that with everyone you meet can you? Come on, you have to be realistic."

I laughed, because I understand what she is saying. How do we have time to connect with everyone we meet? I said, "It doesn't take more time to connect with people. I guess I could have played a game on my phone while you were in the restroom, but instead, I decided to connect with someone sitting next to me."

She said, "But everybody?"

I said, "Well, no. Not everybody. If a person looks like they are studying for a test, I usually just pass on by."

My wife asked me, "But what if the person down the street is a serial killer, should I connect with him?"

I said, "No honey, you only have to connect with people you want to connect to. If you don't want to connect to a serial killer, then by all means, don't."

However, she brings up a good point. Please understand, I am not telling you to connect with every person. And, I am not saying you should never have an opinion or a judgement. It is a good thing to have an opinion and a judgement if a serial killer lives on your block. Be safe, and don't connect to people you feel may be dangerous.

I'm talking about the everyday people we meet. Maybe it's in the office or at the workplace. Maybe it's at the store or the café. Maybe it's in your home with your children and your family.

Remember the time I was washing the glass door at the conference? I connected with a school teacher while I was cleaning the glass door. The teacher said I saved her life. And the connection between us made my day memorable. We were both inspired to greatness!"

There are a many times throughout the day when we worry about things or think about things that aren't present to the moment. We get caught in the same spiral of thoughts that don't bring us any satisfaction. Our brains lead us into thoughts that don't allow us to be present to the current moment. Once I become present to the moment, I realize I have plenty of time to make a connection.

Making connections doesn't put a strain on my schedule. It actually frees up my schedule. I didn't realize how much time I wasted not being present to the moment. Being present frees up my time. I get more done.

I can connect with someone while training them at work. I can connect with a child while cooking at home. I can connect with a neighbor while I'm pulling weeds in my garden. And I can connect with a clerk at a store. I can connect while doing an audit and I can connect during an interrogation. It's not that hard.

My wife asked, "What about in an elevator?"

I said, "Okay. Yes. But it has to be done quickly."

The other day I saw a young man helping an older lady onto an elevator and I quickly created the young man as extraordinary and the moment as very important. I said, "Is this your grandmother?"

He said, "Yes."

I said, "I want to acknowledge you for your virtue of kindness towards your grandmother."

They both smiled and said, "Thank you."

The grandmother then said, "He's a fine young man." The young boy smiled again. The door opened and we left in different directions.

So, yes. In an elevator. Create people you see as extraordinary and the moment as important. And, with ease, you will do what is important.

I often go to the Veteran's Administration Hospital with my father who is a WWII veteran. When I meet people there I usually ask, "When did you serve?" I acknowledge them by saying, "Thank you for your service!" It just seems more impactful than saying, "How are you?"

This really doesn't take any more time, but it slows my day down. Connection allows me to be impactful with people. Connection gives me the avenue to make a difference in people's lives right now. I can enjoy my work, whatever I'm doing, and I can make a difference at work all day long. I don't have to wait until I am rich and retired so I have extra time or money to make a difference in the world.

I can make a difference each and every day. Right now. Listen and lead. Make other people look good.

Five: Acknowledge Them

(How to Connect)

Recognize people for the virtues and values you see in them.

Finally. The exciting part of the five step process!

If you were invited to dinner at a neighbor's home, when you were ready to leave you would thank your neighbor for the wonderful meal and evening. If someone invited you to go to a movie, and they paid for the tickets, you would most likely thank them for making your night fun. You would let them know how much you enjoyed yourself.

Acknowledging someone is basically the same thing. You simply thank them for the difference they made in your life.

If you truly think the other person is extraordinary and you saw some virtues and values you admired, make sure you tell them about what you saw.

If you saw someone volunteer at a homeless shelter, you might say, "Thank you for your service to the homeless. You are making a difference in the world."

If you met a person who colored their hair the same as their grandmother's in honor of their grandma's life... and was going to school to get a degree in business so they could open an orphanage, because their grandma adopted them, you might say something like, "Wow, this is the greatest love story I have ever heard!"

To Summarize:
You already (1.) think the person before you is extraordinary, because you created them as extraordinary. (2.) You realize this is a very important moment because that's how you created it. (3.) You just searched for their virtues and values, and you (4.) listened to them and led the conversation so they looked good. Now you simply (5.) recognize them for the virtues you saw, the values they have and the extraordinary human being they are!

If you are working at the counter at customer service and a customer is upset, it would be fairly easy to see that they have the virtue of fairness. You could listen and lead the conversation by saying, "Thank you for bringing this to our attention. I see that you have the virtue of fairness. What do you think would be fair?"

You might think that people would take advantage of this, but in my experience people are conscientious about being fair after you've recognize the virtue of fairness in them. You cannot just say, "What do you think is fair?" You must first recognize them for the virtue of fairness. After you've solved the problem you can acknowledge them by saying, "Thank you! You helped us solve a problem and you are making us better at serving our guests."

I will finish this chapter with a story.

I was at a conference and an acquaintance of mine came up to me and said, "I heard you are writing a book. What it is about?"

I said, "Well, let me show you."

She said, "Okay, but hurry. I've only got a minute and a half."

I asked, "Where do you live?" And she told me.

I asked, "Why do you live there?"

"So I can have animals," she said.

"What do you like best about having animals?" I asked.

She responded, "Because I like chores."

I asked, "What's your favorite chore?"

She said, "Collecting eggs."

I asked, "Is there someone you're fond of that you used to collect eggs with?"

In a choked up voice, as a tear ran down her face she said, "Yes, my grandpa."

I said, "I want to acknowledge you for your love for your grandpa. You have built your entire home life, where you live, and what you do at home around your love for your grandpa. That's an amazing love story. You must really love your grandpa."

She said, "Thank you. Yes, I do love my grandpa."

Once you hear a love story like the one I just told, simply acknowledge them for it. (Sort of like you would acknowledge someone for an award.) I saw something in her that inspired me, so I simply acknowledged her for it.

I grew up on a farm. I used to collect eggs with my grandpa. And I sure do love my grandpa! But had I related to her on the subject of farms, I would have missed her love for her grandpa. We would have exchanged stories of chores on farms. Exchanging stories of chores on farms would have been nice, but we would never have connected like we did.

I was able to see her heart and her love for her grandpa in less than ninety seconds.

This woman is an extraordinary person. She spent 20 years in the military. If you want something done quickly, efficiently and at a 100% success rate, she's the person to ask. I've never seen her being emotional, except that one time when I connected with her over her love for her grandpa.

Acknowledging people is fairly simple. "Thank you for the amazing dinner." Or, "Thank you for sharing about your love for your grandpa."

Then, you can personalize it a little. "Thank you for the amazing dinner. I had a lovely evening." Or, "Thank you for sharing about your love for your grandpa. What an amazing love story!"

Dale Reeves

Putting it all together

(The Reeves Connection Method)

Usually, when we have a conversation we share something and the person we're with shares something. We share a few opinions to see if they are impressed with us and our intellect. Then we share a few judgments such as, "Can you believe they did that?" Maybe we add in a few complaints about other people or things.

While we are having a conversation with someone we normally look for something to relate to. We think if we've done something similar to what they've done, it will be a special connection. We may think that if we took a vacation in the same country they did, we should relate because that will draw us closer together.

If we find out that we used to live in the same state as them it will be special! I'm sorry to tell you, but a lot of people live in the same state. Just because people live in the same state doesn't mean all of them like each other.

Our conversations often lack something. We don't feel fulfilled at the end of the day. Our conversations didn't really go anyplace special. Nobody was inspired or moved to greatness. We think we did all the right things. We related to the people we spoke with. We gave our opinions to them, and we even gave them advice when we thought they needed it. We shared a few judgments with them, but we just didn't seem to connect on a personal level.

There is a better way to communicate. I call it the Reeves Connection Method. This personal connection method actually moves and inspires people. It creates meaningful and memorable conversations. It creates a bond that is not soon forgotten. It helps me to succeed at home and in business. It makes my life more vivid and full of color. It helps me see just how amazing and extraordinary the people are who share this planet with me!

Sometimes people do things that irritate me, but I create the person as extraordinary anyway. Every life is extraordinary, even if they do things we consider irritating, or even bad.

We can go through life focused on the irritating things people do, and we will find plenty of them. Or we can make a choice to focus on what's extraordinary about people.

The Reeves Connection Method creates a true connection between two people and it inspires people to greatness. It's a fairly simple process.

Let me explain with a final story:

I observed an attendant, Kathy, giving great service at the self-checkout lanes. Giving great customer service is an excellent way to prevent theft while at the same time giving your customers a great experience.

I approached Kathy and said to her, "Wow! You're really giving great customer service! What is it that causes you to give such great customer service?" I wanted to know what her thoughts were about customer service. I thought maybe I could learn something from her that I could use to train other checkers.

She replied, "Well, that's about all I can do."

I was a little shocked by Kathy's statement so I asked, "What do you mean by that?"

She said, "About a year ago I lost all my memory and I can't do very many things. About all I can do is treat people nicely."

I asked, "What was that like, to lose all your memory?"

She said, "I was really terrified."

"Tell me about the first day," I said.

She replied, "I woke up in the hospital. Some people approached me and I didn't know who they were. They called me mom and I didn't even remember that I had any children!"

I said, "That does sound terrifying. How did you get through that?" She shrugged her shoulders.

Then I asked, "What was the first week like?"

She said, "I stayed in the hospital for a while and then they sent me home."

I asked, "What was it like when you got out of the hospital?"

She paused and then replied, "I didn't remember where I lived. When I walked in my house, I didn't know where my room was."

I asked, "What happened then?"

She said, "I had a lot of doctors' appointments and then they brought me to where I worked. Here. The people at work were very patient with me. They told me to take my time and come back when I felt I was ready. So I waited quite a while and I just came back a few months ago. I don't remember much about my job. But I can be nice to people and give good customer service. So that is what I do."

I said, "Wow! I want to acknowledge you for your bravery! Most people would have given up, but you came back. We are blessed to have you working here. That's an extraordinary story. I am glad you came back!"

I walked away and she went back to her work giving great customer service.

We probably talked for only about three minutes.

I came back to the same store the following week. As I walked in the front door of the store the store director came up to me. Then all of a sudden Kathy, the lady who lost her memory, came running up to me and gave me a big hug. She said, "You are my hero!" Then she went back to work.

The store director said, "I don't know what you did to Kathy, but she is a completely different person! And she said it was all because of you."

I said, "Tell me about it. What happened?"

The store director told me that Kathy came to the store on her day off last week and said, "I am here today because of Dale. This is the first time I have left the house other than going to therapy or work, and it's all because of Dale. I'm going to enjoy shopping today."

The store director asked, "What did you do to her?"

I said, "I just listened to her for about three minutes."

The store director said, "Kathy is happier and more productive since you spoke with her. She's really become amazing at her job this past week."

Recalling the day I first saw Kathy, as I approached her, I told myself that this was an extraordinary person. I told myself this was an important moment. I searched for Kathy's virtues and values and it was easy to see bravery. I listened and led the conversation so she could look good. Then I simply acknowledged her for the virtue and value I found in her. That's the five steps. It only took about three minutes.

My father has lost his memory. I could have related and said, "My father has lost a lot of his memory too." But what would that have proved? If I had related I would never have seen her bravery. I refused to relate.

I could have given her advice such as, "My father takes fish oil and it seems to help him. Have you tried that?"

Isn't that what we do sometimes? We give advice on the latest supplement we've tried. Again, she didn't need my advice. I refused to give her advice when the temptation arose.

Kathy still smiles when I go to her store and she gives me big hugs. Since that day when I spoke to her there is a quickness in her step and a bounce in her personality. She's an incredible person. I would have missed the opportunity to hear her story and inspire her to greatness, if I had not taken three minutes to connect with her. Both her life and mine were inspired to greatness.

All she needed was someone to listen to her and to see the real person she is. I only needed to invest three minutes in our conversation! Do you have three minutes today to connect with someone?

You just learned the five steps to the Reeves Connection Method. Now you know how to inspire people to greatness.

Summary of the Reeves Connection Method

Three things to stop doing (The DO-NOT List):

Do not relate. Relating narrows the conversation down to only what two people have in common. Relating is an unproductive habit that inhibits connection.

Do not give an Opinion. Opinions are good. However, opinions separate you from the other person. Opinions draw a line in the sand. If you want to make a connection, don't focus on your differences with the other person. We don't like it when people give us advice. If you want to give advice to others, ask permission to give advice.

Do not judge. Making a judgment puts a wall between you and the person you desire to connect to. Possibly that is why we don't connect with our teenagers. Maybe they feel judged. Connection will not happen if judgment is present. Do not judge based on evidence. You will find what you look for. We usually find evidence to support our judgements. There is a judge, and it isn't you or me. (Unless of course, you are a judge.)

Five steps to connection:

1. **Create the other person as extraordinary.** Without judgments or evidence of any kind, see the other person as amazing and extraordinary. I desire to connect with this person simply because they are extraordinary. They are exactly as I have created them, extraordinary.

2. Create this moment as **a very important moment**. Why? Because it's all we ever have. We only get one moment at a time. It is always very important. Be present to this moment. Time doesn't exist except as a concept. Time exists in the form of a time-measuring-ruler. You can measure time, but you can't save it for later. You only have this moment. I create this moment as very important. Like the first time I looked into my child's eyes and realized that there was a real person looking back at me. Time seems to slow down in that very important moment of finding something extraordinary.

3. **Search for virtues and values**. You will find what you look for. Aim your listening. If you don't find a virtue or value in someone, give them one. You will find what you search for. I desire to search for other people's virtues and values.

4. **Listen and Lead.** Your job is to make the other person shine. Make them look good. The key word here is *listen*. Don't add your opinions or try to relate, but instead, listen for their story and lead them by asking questions about their experiences. Ask deeper questions about what they are talking about. You will have temptations to relate and give opinions. Just ignore those temptations and keep listening and leading. Don't let them ramble on. Be assertive and kind. I desire to listen and lead the conversation because I want to see the beauty the other person has in their personality.

5. **Acknowledge them**. "I acknowledge you for your integrity. This world needs more people like you." "Thank you for your service to our country. I am safe because of you." Let them know the virtue and value you see in them. You don't have to use the word, "Acknowledge." "Just say thank you for your kindness." Or, "That's an amazing love story." I desire to acknowledge other people for the positive impact they've had on me. I desire to acknowledge people for the positive impact they have on other people's lives.

Final Thoughts

I always have at least one witness, also called an observer, sitting in the same room with me during my interrogations. A number of years ago, after conducting an interrogation I had an observer ask me, "How did you do that? How did you take this guy who's belligerent, cocky and upset and get him to willingly confess and to want to take responsibility for what he did? How did you stay so calm during the whole process? I know I would have started yelling at him! But you calmly helped him admit to his theft, write a confession, sign his confession and then he thanked you for helping him! How did you do that?"

I tried to explain to the observer all of the principles that I follow to make me successful. I could tell by the puzzled look on the observer's face that my explanation seemed a little complicated to him. This was when I began to write down the Reeves Connection Method in an easier to understand model. That's where this book came from. I'm excited to share these principles with you!

If you've attended one of my seminars, thank you for who you are and for sharing your presence with me. Every time I conduct a seminar, I am inspired by the lives of the people attending. You have enriched my life. It is an amazing experience to connect with you and to see the richness of the virtues you have and the value you bring to the world.

To my readers, thank you for the time you spent reading this book. I have enjoyed sharing my passion for this subject with you. I would thoroughly enjoy hearing about your struggles and triumphs as you put the Reeves Connection Method into practice.

I know that in this book I have presented a number of concepts that, at first, may seem strange and foreign to the ways we've been taught to think. Concepts such as:

Time does not exist.

Do not relate.

What if nothing's wrong?

If you don't see a virtue or value, give them one.

If you are like me, I questioned these concepts at first. It took a while for me to get out of the old style of communication that I was entrenched in. But after applying these concepts to my life over and over again, they started to make complete sense to me.

Maybe I had the 'luxury' of being forced to have very intense conversations during my interrogations. Maybe this forced me to study my conversations and figure out how to be more successful in connecting with someone.

Obviously, I have learned from my failures. But after studying my interrogations and many of my everyday conversations, I saw these concepts were successful. As I applied these concepts to my life, they transformed my life into something totally different. When I was living 'life as usual' I never knew how trapped I was in the unsatisfying 'nice' conversations I had all day. I never knew all that I was missing. I would never go back to 'life as usual!' Now, my life is extraordinary, my relationships are extraordinary and the people I meet are extraordinary.

My challenge to you is simple. Try these concepts out one at a time. Start with, do not relate. See what happens. Then tell yourself every morning, I create this day as very important. I create this day as the best day I've ever had." Upon meeting somebody, tell yourself that you create this person as extraordinary. Study your conversations and the results. Read the list of virtues again, and then complete the worksheet for a few people in your life. Slowly and surely, one concept at a time, you will clearly see how this transforms your life into something you will love.

When we create understanding, everything changes. In my story with Tommy, I created understanding between us.

Tommy understands that his grades need to improve and he understands that I want to know what is going on at school. Tommy also understands that I admire him and that I value a relationship with him. After listening to Tommy, I understand what's going on with Tommy at school. I take what is potentially a high-conflict situation and turn it into a clear understanding that actually builds a relationship between us.

Imagine a world where everyone connected! I ask for your partnership. If I can bring connection to some of the most confrontational conversations, then you can help me bring it to the world, one conversation at a time.

Author   Dale Norman Reeves, CFI

Sometimes people ask, "What does the CFI after your name mean?" CFI stands for Certified Forensic Interviewer. CFI is a certification standard for experienced interviewers.

If you wish to leave comments or if you would like to contact me to give a seminar or conduct training sessions, you may do so by sending me an email at reevesconnectionmethod@outlook.com

Acknowledgements

I would like to acknowledge and thank my family members and friends who gave me feedback on the chapters of this book. Thank you for your generous time and candid feedback. I want to thank my family for your patience and encouragement for the many hours I have worked on this book! I want to thank those people who have attended one of my seminars and acknowledge the participants in my public speaking career, those who found the information valuable and for the feedback I have received. Thank you also to the people who asked me, "Do you have a book?" And, when I said, "No." asked me, "Well, when are you going to write one?" Here it is. With love to each of you, Dale Norman Reeves, CFI.

Dale Reeves

48151329R00136

Made in the USA
San Bernardino, CA
18 April 2017